D0876336

HERBS

Edible

Series Editor: Andrew F. Smith

EDIBLE is a revolutionary new series of books dedicated to food and drink that explores the rich history of cuisine. Each book reveals the global history and culture of one type of food or beverage.

Already published

Herbs

A Global History

Gary Allen

REAKTION BOOKS

For J. V. Allen (1924–2010)

Published by Reaktion Books Ltd
33 Great Sutton Street
London EC1V 0DX, UK
www.reaktionbooks.co.uk

First published 2012

Printed and bound in China by C&C Offset Printing Co., Ltd

British Library Cataloguing in Publication Data
Allen, Gary
Herbs : a global history. – (Edible)
1. Herbs. 2. Cooking (Herbs) – History.
3. Cooking (Herbs)
I. Title II. Series
641.6′57′09-DC23

ISBN 978 1 86189 925 5

Contents

Introduction

Long before humans began to cultivate their own crops, they hunted and foraged for food. Eventually they found that they could produce larger quantities of grains and vegetables through farming, but the plants that made their meals more interesting still grew wild in the rocky places that were unsuitable to cereal agriculture. The plants that we call 'herbs' continued to be hunted in the wild – indeed, in many parts of the world they still are.

Early farmers learned that, for their fields to remain fertile, they needed periodic rests – or fallow periods. The ancient Hebrews even made this part of their laws. Leviticus 25:2–5 and 20–22 specify that every seventh year the fields could not be planted. During that year, people tended to revert to a kind of hunter-gatherer existence, during which wild plants were especially esteemed. The Talmud even helped by distinguishing between wild and domesticated versions of the same plants, giving distinctive names to the wild versions (which included rocket (arugula), celery, chicory, coriander (cilantro), mustard, purslane and rue).[1]

Gradually, many of these savoury weeds began to be planted in small household gardens, usually within easy reach of the person who did the cooking.

[Some] years ago, an archaeologist noticed some Rosemary growing in an oddly regular fashion. Digging 10–12 feet below the surface, he discovered the ruins of a small house. Some ancient Roman had planted the Rosemary conveniently close to the kitchen door. Long after the occupants had passed on to their culinary rewards, and their house crumbled, the Rosemary lived on. Century after century, the soil built up over the spot, rising slowly enough for the Rosemary to keep its head above the horizon.[2]

Some small kitchen gardens eventually evolved into formal herb gardens. It is no accident that herbs, those glorified weeds, are grown in the only food gardens that are designed for their aesthetic properties. While all other crops are grown for efficiency of production, these lowly weeds have a place of honour, close to our homes and hearts. Herb gardens are intended to appeal to all of our senses, to encourage us to linger in their intimate, civilized wildness. Sometimes these 'weeds' can be found thriving in pots on our kitchen windowsills.

Herbs have been with us since before we were modern humans. They have evolved with us – like cats and dogs – and, just as our pets have become family members, we like to pamper them and keep them close because these plants retain just enough of their original wildness to endlessly fascinate us.

I

What, Exactly, Are Herbs?

It's a frequently asked question. It would be wonderful to have a simple and straightforward answer but, unfortunately, no such answer exists. Part of the problem is that the word 'herb' means different things to different people.

'Spice' means nothing at all to botanists, and when they think of herbs they mean non-woody vascular plants that die, or at least waste away, after flowering. Most cooks, and many gardeners, would find that definition essentially useless. For one thing, they've noticed that some 'herbs' can with age become woody – which means the stems are tough enough to survive frost without melting away as annuals do, and are similar to the twigs of a tree – and don't actually 'waste away' (for example: rosemary, sage and thyme).

Cooks often distinguish herbs from spices by the part of the plant used in cooking: 'herbs' are foliage or flowers, while 'spices' consist of bark, seeds and roots. In practice, at least in the European tradition, 'herbs' are parts of plants that are grown in domestic gardens, while spices are almost always imported – usually from tropical parts of the globe. Unfortunately, no matter which set of rules one chooses, it is bound to have so many exceptions that its usefulness is questionable.

For example, mustard (*Brassica* and *Sinapis* spp.) and coriander (*Coriandrum sativum*) seeds are treated like spices but they thrive in temperate gardens, and both produce foliage that is used more like the ingredients we call 'herbs'. Young mustard leaves are eaten as a salad herb, while older leaves are cooked slowly, as pot-herbs. Coriander leaves, cilantro, are used sparingly as a fresh herb in many cuisines (indeed, in Thai kitchens the leaves, stems and roots are considered to be different ingredients, and have distinct names). In some places, like Vietnam, coriander is used by the handful – it's practically a vegetable.

We also use several different terms to categorize the plants, and parts thereof, we use in our kitchens. We have already seen salad herbs and pot-herbs, but there are also herbal teas (infusions that are better described as tisanes). Some of these

Assorted herbs (basil, Italian flat-leaf parsley, sage, tarragon and thyme) from the author's garden.

Coriander, or cilantro (*Coriandrum sativum*). The newest (more finely dissected) leaves at the top of each sprig indicate that the plant is about to go to seed.

plants and plant parts serve primarily as 'seasoning', while others do not. This is not a problem for English speakers only. In Germany, 'kraut' refers to any ingredient based on leafy plant matter; 'sauerkraut' is probably familiar to everyone, but 'bohnenkraut' may not be – the word means 'bean herb' and it's used for both summer and winter savory (*Satureja* spp.). Chinese cooks are heavily dependent upon a number of fermented ingredients to add flavour to their dishes, but use only a couple of spices, and perhaps three herbs, as seasoning. However, their cooking features a large variety of leafy greens we would consider to be pot-herbs. The Vietnamese, as noted above, use leafy plants we would describe as 'culinary herbs' in such large quantities that they seem like salad greens – rather intensely flavoured, to be sure, but 'salad' nonetheless.

Virtually every reference describes cloves as a 'spice', yet they are the unopened buds of flowers – which, by conventional logic, suggests that they should be listed among the herbs. While Europeans only know the dried flower buds of this tropical evergreen tree, an Indonesian might use its leaves, twigs and bark. The clove tree provides seasoning, food, perfume and even cigarettes called *kretek*, all made with one or more parts of the tree. The Eurocentric term 'spice' seems wholly inadequate when seen from the perspective of the Indonesians who harvest it.

What we choose to call 'herbs' and 'spices' are often little more than accidents of geography, history and contemporary modes of transportation. Many of the ingredients we call 'herbs' are parts of plants which traditionally have been grown in European gardens. Before the Age of Exploration 'spices' could only be obtained through a series of intermediaries who, for commercial reasons, preferred to keep the knowledge of their sources proprietary. These sources were so mysterious to European consumers that many believed that they grew only in the Garden of Eden. Since cinnamon, cloves, ginger and pepper could not be grown in Europe's temperate climate, they were imported from distant lands, on the backs of camels that trudged along secret spice routes, or, later, on very small ships. The spices changed hands many times along the way (the price rising at every step, an early example of what we would describe as 'value added' today). The costs imposed by the spice traders and the dangers they faced along the way forced them to choose only the most densely flavoured parts of tropical plants. Handling large amounts of leaves and twigs was simply not cost-effective.

If the discussion of herbs and spices has told us anything, it is that distinguishing between them is troublesome. While most of us are certain that cinnamon is a spice (it is the inner bark of a tropical tree, and its flavour and aroma are intense), the ancient Greeks and Romans had a different take altogether. They imported vast quantities of leaves they called *phyllon* and *malabathrum*, which came from a tree that is closely related to the one that gives us cinnamon (*malabathrum* is *Cinnamomum tamala*, while true cinnamon is *C. zeylanicum*). These leaves have an even stronger cinnamon quality than the bark, so perhaps we should be asking ourselves why the use of these leaves died out. One answer is that it didn't – it's still commonly used in the cooking of South Asia (Bhutan, India and Nepal).

Simply put, herbs are all those plant parts – other than spices (given the caveat that the definition of 'spices' is less than clear) – that we use to enhance our food. Traditionally, Europeans and emigrants from Europe have used the term 'herbs' for those plant products – used to add flavour and scent to their dishes – they could grow for themselves. 'Spices' were used the same way, but were always imported, and hence more expensive. This led to the perception that spices were somehow more prestigious than herbs – which, in turn, led to the use of spices in court, or *haute*, cuisine. Herbs tended to be seen as common everyday ingredients, more suitable for ordinary meals.

This difference of approach is arbitrary, based on class distinction, and has nothing to do with the ingredients themselves. In today's world, the expense of shipping ingredients from distant shores has been reduced to the point where economic considerations are irrelevant. While clarifying the precise divisions between herbs and spices may be difficult, what is certain is that we value all of these plant parts because they contain small but intense quantities of alcohols, aldehydes, acids, alkaloids, essential oils, esters, ethers, terpenoids and so on, which add flavour and aroma to our foods. In today's kitchens, the only real difference between herbs and spices is the concentration of the flavouring compounds they contain. Spices are invariably stronger, and tend to be added to dishes earlier to extract as much flavour as possible. Herbs, especially fresh herbs, tend to be added later in cooking, so that volatile flavours and aromas are not lost before serving.

While we're discussing the chemicals that give herbs their distinctive tastes and aromas we should correct a popular misconception – one that has been repeated in countless recipe books. We are often told that, in substituting dried herbs for fresh, we should reduce the amount used to one-third of the original recommendation. That may be true for some herbs, but as a guiding principle it has some serious drawbacks. When herbs dry, they tend to lose some of their volatile compounds. If they lost them in any sort of consistent manner, there might be some use to the general rule of substitution. However, not all herbs are so dependable. Some herbs become stronger when dried, some do not. Some compounds are altered into different compounds as they dry (due to fermentation or other chemical processes). Again, some essential compounds are more volatile than others. These variables can produce a stronger-flavoured herb, a weaker one or a totally different one.

For example, fresh tarragon has a lovely anise-like scent due to the presence of anisol. Unfortunately, when the leaves lose their water, they also lose much of their anisol – so their hint of liquorice is greatly diminished. At the same time, a bit of fermentation causes other compounds in the leaves to convert to coumarin, which gives dried tarragon the pleasant – but different – scent of new-mown hay.[1]

When substituting dried herbs for fresh, we must consider not only the amount to be used, but also the fact that the substitute is actually a different ingredient from that which was originally specified.

Our ancestors may not have known about the chemical compounds that gave herbs their appeal, but that didn't stop them from believing that these plants had medical or magical properties. The Doctrine of Signatures was an ancient notion, now regarded as a superstition, that led people to believe that the appearance of herbs was somehow connected to their medical properties: for example, the leaves of hepaticas resembled the liver, so were thought to be beneficial to that organ. Some herbs actually *do* have medical properties, but that's beyond the scope of this book. For us, the magic that they add to our tables is more than enough reason to study them, their origins and their spread around the globe.

One final issue must be addressed. While we put aside our confusion about what are, or are not, herbs, the names we have given these plants is another story. Common names for plants (and birds, fish, animals and so on) are notoriously troublesome. Many completely different species often share the same or similar common names. This is not surprising,

Otto Brunfels, 'Hepatica' (*Hepatica* spp.), from *Herbarium Vivae Eicones* (1530), engraving.

since different plants may serve the same culinary function and be treated as if they were the same species. Sometimes a new plant, in a new place, simply reminded someone of a familiar plant in the old country. To try to minimize such confusions, botanists prefer to use the Latin binomial system invented by Linnaeus. It may seem pedantic and overly fussy, but it's the best method we have to be clear about the plants we're discussing. Unfortunately, even the binomial system has its weaknesses.

Science is an ever-changing field. As scientists learn more about the connections – and differences – among species, taxonomists (the people responsible for the naming and categorizing of species) sometimes have to change the scientific names given to plants. Since Linnaeus began the process of systemizing the entire living world, back in the eighteenth century, a lot of science has changed. Consequently, many of the useful terms we used to use to categorize plants have been changed, eliminated, subdivided or recombined with others and, as a result – especially if one consults older texts (such as herbals) – the exact identity of the plants that interest us is occasionally uncertain.

A rational person might suspect that for a system of taxonomy to be successful, universality is a key requirement. Such a person is bound to be disappointed. Successive generations

Round-lobed hepatica (*Hepatica americana*), a wild native plant in New York's Dutchess County.

of scientists have often chosen to change the system, sometimes for very good reasons – but not everyone adopts the changes. Different authors, in different places, have elected to incorporate some, all or none of the changes made by others. As a result, a single species might have several different scientific names. It might be listed in several different genera. It might even appear in more than one family. All we can do is try to use the most recent names available, acknowledge the changes when we can and understand that our best efforts will probably go awry within a generation or less.

2

The Usual Suspects

Most herb books focus on a dozen or so species, which just happen to grow in European herb gardens and consequently are over-represented in the literature of herbs. In the past, herbs served many uses outside of the kitchen, so early herbals tend to feature vast amounts of facts – or imagined facts – that are of no use to a modern cook or gardener. For the purposes of this book such impedimenta will be ignored – unless, of course, they are so charmingly quaint and silly that we can't resist including them.

Early Cookbooks

The earliest surviving cookbook (falsely attributed to a first-century Roman gourmet named Apicius) is *De Re Coquinaria*. Obviously, people were cooking, and presumably using recipes, long before that. A few scraps of recipes have come down to us from the third century BCE, from a Syracusan Greek named Mithekos, who was described as 'the Phidias of Cooking' after the most famous sculptor of the ancient world.[1] In fact, not long ago the French historian Jean Bottéro went even farther back by translating a few proto-recipes on

Mesopotamian cuneiform tablets that had long been part of a collection at Yale University. These are recipes for dishes that are almost recognizable or at least can be imagined on today's tables.[2] Mesopotamian pantries were similar to those of modern Middle Eastern kitchens, minus grapes, olives and of course anything from the New World. They included familiar herbs such as rocket (arugula), dill, coriander, cress, fennel, marjoram, mint, mustard, rosemary, rue, saffron and thyme,[3] and still-unidentified herbs called *sahlu* and *zurumu*.[4]

Clay tablets from Mycenaean Greece – the period some 3,500 years ago described by Homer – mention herbs in use at the time: celery, coriander, fennel and mint. We don't know if they were used as food, medicine or perfume, a confusion that still exists today.[5]

Early Herbalists

The earliest herbal texts were less concerned with cooking than with medical usage (which is not surprising, since the earliest surviving cookbook, *De Re Coquinaria*, didn't appear until the fourth century CE).

In the second century BCE Theophrastus of Athens wrote his *Historia Plantarum*, a ten-volume encyclopedia of botany that included the rough beginnings of taxonomy and an approach to describing plants based on features that foreshadowed Linnaeus by some 2,000 years. He categorized plants according to the form of their roots and leaves, while we tend to use details of their reproductive organs, flowers, instead. Together, Aristotle and Theophrastus studied the botany of the Greek island of Lesbos.

Pliny the Elder compiled his encyclopedia of the natural world, *Natural History*, in the first century CE. Here he assembled

160 volumes of notes on what was known (or believed to be known) about everything that lived, grew or merely existed in the physical world. The exact date of completion is unknown but, since he perished while observing the eruption of Vesuvius that buried Pompeii and Herculaneum, we know it had to be before 25 August, CE 79. His encyclopedia is divided into 37 books, with books 12–27 devoted to botany (and subgenres of agriculture, horticulture and pharmacology). He borrowed directly from Theophrastus, including the patently ridiculous ideas that basil 'when old, degenerates into wild thyme' or that 'plants, indeed, will turn of a yellow complexion on the approach of a woman who has the menstrual discharge upon her'.[6] He also made use of *De Re Rustica*, an agricultural treatise by his contemporary, Lucius Junius Moderatus Columella.

The five volumes of Pedanius Dioscorides' *De Materia Medica* (CE 65) catalogued over 600 plants. The first volume dealt with the properties (including culinary properties) of herbs. He organized the plants according to their attributes and characteristics, rather than alphabetically, which he felt arbitrarily destroyed meaningful relationships. This is essentially what modern botanists do; characteristics define the relationships between species, and those that share such characteristics are grouped together within genera, families and so on.

Nonetheless, copyists spent much of the next 1,500 years rearranging the entries, often substituting convenience for reason. *De Materia Medica* was the standard text until the late Middle Ages, in fact until the works of Galen were rediscovered in the Renaissance. Much of what we know about Egyptian herbs is based on 120 Egyptian names for herbs collected in *De Materia Medica*. Many of these terms seem to be made up (and probably were, a century after the death of Dioscorides), but some appear to name herbs that are still use today (celery, *mith*; chicory and endive, *agon*; coriander, *okhion*; cress, *semeth*; dill, *arakhou*; elecampane, *lenis*; fenugreek, *itasin*; garden orach, *asaraphi*; horehound, *asterispa*; marjoram, *sopho*; purslane, *mekhmoutim*; sage, *apousi*; and wormwood, *somi*). Egyptians recognized at least three different mints: curly mint, *Mentha torgifolia*; water mint, *M. sativa*; and peppermint, *M. piperita*, naming them *bellou*, *makitho* and *tis*, respectively. The savory used by Egyptians was *Satureja thymbra* (*sekemene*); their thyme was *Thymus sibthorpii* (*meroupyos*). Dioscorides did not include an Egyptian name for parsley – he merely listed it as 'mountain celery'.

'Apicius' is a name associated with a great gourmet in first-century Rome who is alleged to have chosen suicide over a life in which his finances might not have allowed him to go on eating in the grandest style. The collection of recipes that bear his name in *De Re Coquinaria* were compiled some 300 years after any of the possible Apicii flourished (four different people named Apicius are candidates for the honour of first cookbook author, even though none of them actually wrote the book). The book features a number of culinary herbs. Some of them are recognizable today and still in use in modern kitchens (*porrum*, leek; *ligusticum*, lovage; *petrosilenium*, parsley). Some are harder to identify (*laser*, asafoedita; *malabathrum*, leaves of a close relative of cinnamon; *nardostachyum*, spikenard) and some incorporate ingredients from plants that are now extinct (*silphium*). The last plant, silphium, was so popular both as a culinary herb and as a contraceptive (though its effectiveness as the latter was probably wishful thinking) that the Romans used up the last of them by the beginning of the first century of the modern era. Pliny, who regarded it as 'one of the most precious gifts of Nature to man', wrote that only one stalk of silphium of Cyrenaica (now part of the Libyan coast) had been found in his lifetime.

Apuleius Platonicus, chervil (*Chaerophyllum bulbosum*), water mint (*Mentha aquatica*), alexanders (*Smyrnium olusatrum*), lily (*Lilium candidum*), spurge (*Euphorbia* sp.), from *Herbarium* (1431), engraving.

Apuleius Platonicus, 'Physician Gathering Herbs', from *Herbarium*,
c. 1200.

The *Herbarium* (fifth century CE) of Apuleius Platonicus (also known as Lucius Apuleius of Madaura and Pseudo-Apuleius) drew on data extracted from Pliny, Theophrastus and Dioscorides. His manuscript later became one of the first books to make use of the new printing press. *Herbarium Apuleii Platonici* (1481) was the first printed herb book to feature illustrations. Its success encouraged a host of imitators (*Herbarius Moguntinus*, in Latin, 1484; *Herbarius*, also known as *Gart der Gesundheit*, in German, 1485; and *Hortus Sanitatis*, in Latin, 1491). This was long before copyright was even imagined, so all of these books borrowed freely from classical authors and each other. The *Herbarium* was the first herbal text to appear in England, becoming the model for later texts such as Nicholas Culpeper's *The English Physitian*.

The Grete Herball (1526), while not the first herb book published in England, was the first to feature detailed botanical information. It was based almost entirely on *Herbarius zu Tetsch* (1496) and *Le Grand Herbier* (1520),[7] the former being the precursor to a great flowering of German herbals in the sixteenth and seventeenth centuries. Otto Brunfels's *Herbarium Vivae Eicones* (1530), Leonhart Fuchs's *De Historia Stirpium* (1542), Jerome Bock (Hieronymous Tragus)'s *Kreuter Büch* (1546–51) and Valerius Cordus's *Historia Plantarum* (1544) and *Dispensatorium* (published posthumously, 1546) are the founding works of German botany.[8] These books have fine woodcut illustrations and those in the 1545 edition of Fuchs's book were extensively copied in later herbals (such as *A New Herball*, Turner, 1551–68; *Crüydeboeck*, Dodoens, 1554; *Nieve Herball*, Lyte, 1578; *Historia Plantarum Universalis*, Bauhin, 1650; *Anleitung*, Schinz, 1774).[9] Charles Estienne's *Agriculture et maison rustique* (1564) was the first book on the subject, written in French. In it he recommends that herb gardens should contain many scented herbs, including balm,

Nicholas Culpeper,
from *The English
Physitian* (1652),
engraving.

basil, costmary, hyssop, lavender, marjoram, rosemary, sage
and thyme.

The competition between these herbals to secure what
we would call 'market share' was fierce. Fuchs, for example,
wrote, 'Among all the herbals which exist today, there are none
which have more of the crassest errors than those which
Egenolph, the printer, has already published again and again.'
Egenolph had included, without permission, plates pirated
from Fuchs's book as illustrations for a new edition of *Gart
der Gesundheit* (Fuchs's rant did little to discourage Egenolph's
sales; his publications remained in print for 250 years).[10]

John Gerard's *The Herball, or Generall Historie of Plants* is among the most famous of the early books on the subject. Published in 1597, the book draws upon many of the herbals listed above but adds good descriptions of the plants. Unfortunately, the book also includes a lot of folklore or, as modern food scholars would say, 'fakelore'. To this day, herb books exhibit this tendency, which either charms or exasperates modern readers.

For English-speaking readers, Nicholas Culpeper (1616–1654), while not the first British herbalist, is the real beginning of the herbal tradition. Culpeper was also an astrologer, which

Leonhart Fuchs, from *Der Nieuwer Herbaris*, 1545, engraving.

Leonhart Fuchs, 'Common Plantain' (*Plantago major*), from *De Historia Stirpium* (1542), engraving.

John Gerard, title page of *The Herball*, 1597.

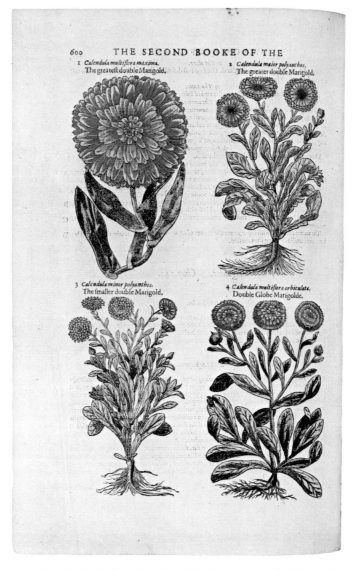

1 *Calendula multiflora maxima.*
The greatest double Marigold.

2 *Calendula maior polyanthos.*
The greater double Marigold.

3 *Calendula minor polyanthos.*
The smaller double Marigold.

4 *Calendula multiflora orbiculata.*
Double Globe Marigolde.

John Gerard, 'Marigolds' (*Calendula officinalis*) from *The Herball*, 16th century.

means his work is an example of a shortcoming often seen in herbal literature: the admixture of arcane notions, such as astrology, alchemy and the Doctrine of Signatures, with useful pragmatically obtained information. His book, *The English Physitian*, better known today as Culpeper's *Herbal* (1652), was carried to the new colonies in North America, primarily as a medical text.

One of the first 'herb' books to focus on the culinary as opposed to the medicinal properties of herbs was John Evelyn's 1699 *Acetaria: A Discourse of Sallets*. The term 'Acetaria' was borrowed from Pliny and referred to a 'vinegar diet', the belief that eating raw cabbages with vinegar made them more healthful and easy to digest. It was followed by Sidney Smith's *An Herb Sallad for the Tavern Bowl* (1796), which featured a

Mandrake, from a Saxon herbal. Mandrake was one of the Doctrine of Signatures' favourite cure-alls. Because its roots were said to resemble a human body, it was said to cure almost any disease.

'Mandrake' (*Mandragora autumnalis*), from *Pflanzenbuch* (Book of Plants, *c.* 1500).

recipe including, 'all lettuces, sorrel, salad burnet, tarragon, lovage, shallots, garlic chives, chervil, watercress and parsley'.[11]

Valerius Cordus was especially significant because, unlike many of his Germanic contemporaries, he travelled to Italy to see at first hand the Mediterranean herbs that were the core of the European herbal tradition. Herbals, even to this day, are prone to repetition of 'facts' (proven or otherwise) that come from older herbal texts. This reliance on authority – as opposed to observation and experiment – should have been rendered obsolete by the new scientific method espoused in Francis Bacon's *Novum Organum* (1620), but somehow survives in much of the herbal literature. This was despite the fact that Culpeper, in his 'Original Epistle to the Reader', wrote:

> I cannot build my faith upon Authors' words, nor believe
> a thing because they say it, and could wish every body
> were of my mind in this – to labour to be able to give a
> reason for every thing they say or do. They say Reason
> makes a man differ from a Beast; if that be true, pray
> what are they that, instead of reason for their judgment,
> quote old Authors?[12]

Other Uses

While we tend to think of herbs as primarily culinary, or as alternative medicines, before modern times they occupied a much larger part of people's everyday lives. For one thing, they were not 'alternative' medicine in the past – before the creation of modern drugs, most of which are entirely synthetic, doctors' entire pharmacopoeia was based on herbs. Some of our drugs are the descendants of early herbal remedies (aspirin is a synthetic variation on extracts from willow bark; 'salicylic acid' refers to the willow genus, *Salix*). Likewise, many of today's botanical names are etymologically connected to the ancient names used by apothecaries. The use of today's alternative medicines reflect a distrust of modern science that sometimes arises from the lack of success of some modern treatments, but also from an urge to connect to a past that is seen as simpler, purer, than the frantic world we now inhabit. One could argue that the Slow Food movement reflects similar motivations.

Whether they were grown in special gardens, or simply gathered in the wild, herbs served a host of uses that have largely disappeared today. At one time they provided virtually all dyestuffs (with the exception of cochineal, which is made from a small aphid-like insect: *Dactylopius coccus*). That changed in 1856 when William Henry Perkin created the first synthetic dye: mauveine. The colour is named for a wild plant of the mallow (*Malva*) family – 'mauve' is French for 'mallow', which had been used as a name for the colour for nearly two centuries. Ironically, Perkin discovered the dyestuff by accident. He had been trying to synthesize a totally different botanical substance from coal-tar (a by-product of the production of the gas used for lighting in the nineteenth century): quinine.

The world was a smellier place in the days before air fresheners came in aerosol cans, and hygiene was practised somewhat less enthusiastically than it is today. We might use botanicals to scent the air in pot pourri or pomanders but we do so because they are charmingly old-fashioned, not because they are particularly effective. Sweet-smelling herbs played a much larger role in the past. Fragrant herbs and flowers were commonly strewn on floors to absorb whatever might have fallen there, to discourage infestations of small vermin and to release their pleasant scents when trod

Peter Schoeffer, 'Coriander' (*Coriandrum sativum*), from *Herbarius Latinus* (1484), engraving.

The aromatic herbs market, Taibei (Taiwan).

upon. Throughout the Middle Ages and the Renaissance aromatic herbs like meadowsweet (*Filipendula ulmaria*), mugwort (*Artemisia vulgaris*), sweet woodruff, rosemary and yarrow served as multi-functional carpets. While peasants tossed wild herbs on the floors of their homes themselves, royal households employed full-time strewers to collect sweet-smelling herbs, spread them around the floors of their castles and remove them after they had lost their freshness.

During the reign of Henry VIII Thomas Tusser listed sixteen other herbs – and a few flowers – that were considered essential for strewers. They included basil (*Ocimum* spp.), camphor or costmary, chamomile (*Anthemis* spp.), fennel, germander (*Teucrium chamaedrys*), hyssop, three different lavenders, lemon balm (*Melissa officinalis*), marjoram (*Origanum majorana*), pennyroyal (*Mentha pulegium*), mints (*Mentha* spp.), sage (*Salvia officinalis*), tansy (*Tanacetum vulgare*) and winter savory (*Satureja montana*).[13]

Strewing was such an important function that King James II created the position of Royal Herb Strewer in the seventeenth century. The position became purely ceremonial after the death of George III, but has been passed down as an honorary title to this day.

The Basics

Early accounts of herbs were largely medical, though occasional culinary mentions of them can be seen. The ancient Egyptians used many herbs, and their names for them have come down to us largely through the work of Theophrastus (372–287 BCE). The foliage of coriander (*Coriandrum sativum*) was called *okhion* by the Ancient Egyptians. Its seeds were carefully placed in Tutankhamun's tomb. Long afterwards, Pliny believed the

Francisco Hernandez,
'Agave' (*Agave* spp),
from *Rerum Medicarum*
(1651), engraving.

best-quality coriander still came from Egypt. Dill (*Anethum graveolens*) was another familiar herb to the ancient Egyptians. The Egyptians called their mustard (*Sinapis arvensis*) *euthmoi*, while their hedge mustard (*Sisymbrium officinalis*) was *erethmou*. Chervil (*Anthriscus cerefolium*) was known and used as early as Egypt's Middle Kingdom; like coriander, a basket of chervil seeds was included in Tutankhamun's tomb for his journey to the afterlife.

Pliny the Elder describes the flowering habit of basil (*Ocimum basilicum*) but his description is so inaccurate that it suggests that he was describing some other plant entirely. Elsewhere, he provides advice that seems utterly ludicrous: basil seeds should be planted 'with the utterance of curses and imprecations, the result being that it grows all the better for it;

the earth, too, is rammed down when it is sown, and prayers offered that the seed may never come up.'[14]

Pliny lumped all members of the allium family together as 'bulbs'. He described varieties from all over the Roman Empire (yet praised squill, *Scilla* spp., most highly, which – among all the alliums – is probably the least eaten today). He mentioned spring onions or scallions as being 'employed for seasonings',[15] as opposed to the use of other alliums as vegetables. Fennel (*Foeniculum vulgare*) was a favourite among the ancient Egyptians, Greeks and Romans. Fennel branches sat under Roman bread while it baked. Hippocrates listed rosemary (*Rosmarinus officinalis*) and sage – which grow wild all around the Mediterranean, and were common in Ancient Egypt – in his *Materia Medica*. He considered mint a useful medical plant.

Rosemary blossoms (*Rosmarinus officinalis*), in the herb gardens of The Culinary Institute of America, Hyde Park, New York.

Pliny wrote about mint, in a more culinary vein, that it is 'used in the dishes at rustic entertainments [and] pervades the tables far and wide with its agreeable odour'. He also noted that 'once planted, it lasts a considerable length of time', a tendency that plagues modern gardeners.[16] Of common thyme (*Thymus vulgaris*) Pliny wrote that '[m]ost mountains abound with wild thyme' and that it was commonly gathered in Greece.[17] Pliny commented that mustard's pungency is 'rendered imperceptible by boiling; the leaves, too, are boiled just the same way as those of other vegetables' (that is, as a pot-herb).[18] His observation was accurate, even if the reason is something he could not have known. The 'hot' compounds (isothiocyanates) in mustard and horseradish are only created when enzymes in the plants react with other compounds in the plant (when cells are broken, allowing the chemicals to

SALVIA
MINOR.

Creüts falbey.

Leonhart Fuchs, 'Sage' (*Salvia officinalis*), from *De Historia Stirpium* (1542), engraving.

Common thyme (*Thymus vulgaris*). This is part of a huge patch that escaped from a garden in Schroon Lake, New York.

react). If these plants are cooked *before* the reaction occurs, heat destroys the enzymes, so no isothiocyanates are formed.

Pliny described parsley (*Petroselinum crispum*) as a salad herb. He devoted much of chapter 17 (Book XIX) to parsley, but several of the plants he described are poisonous members of *Apiaceae*. Pliny suggested using savory with onions, 'the onions being all the finer for it'.[19] Elsewhere, Pliny seems to confuse lovage (*Ligusticum levisticum*) with *satureia*, which has given us the name of the genus for savory (*Satureja*).[20]

Culpeper believed basil was vile and dangerous. His reasoning: 'Something is the matter; this herb and rue will not grow together, no, nor near one another: and we know rue is as great an enemy to poison as any that grows' and he concludes that he 'dare write no more of it'.[21] Nonetheless, basil was used in seventeenth-century England to flavour Fetter Lane sausage. Culpeper called oregano (*Origanum vulgare*) 'wind marjoram' – no doubt meaning 'wild marjoram' – and did not mention a single culinary use for it. Apparently pizza was not part of his regular diet.

Culpeper excused himself from describing the many herbs that were 'so well known that [they] need no description'. Among them were bay leaf (*Laurus nobilis*), winter sweet marjoram or pot marjoram and parsley as well as summer and winter savories (*Satureja* spp.), 'being entertained as constant

Bay leaf (*Laurus nobilis*), here grown in a greenhouse, since it can't withstand northern winters.

Spearmint (*Mentha spicata*) growing on the Clermont Estate, Germantown, New York.

inhabitants in our gardens', needed no description from Culpeper (and, apparently, merited no mention of culinary usage).[22] Rosemary was also ignored – though he was ready to perpetuate the notion that rosemary was good for the memory (he felt the same way about sage) – and tarragon (*Artemisia dracunculus* 'sativa') doesn't even appear in Culpeper. He says just one thing about mint: that it helps 'a stinking breath'.[23]

Mustard's 'round yellowish seed, [is] sharp, hot, and biting upon the tongue', wrote Culpeper (who, when it came to matters gustatory, was always ready to state the obvious).[24]

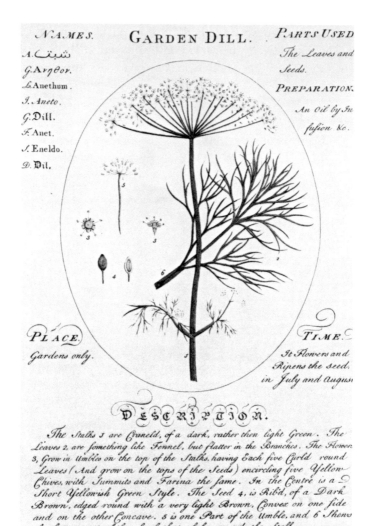

GARDEN DILL.

NAMES.
A. شبت
G. Ἄργθον.
L. Anethum.
J. Aneto.
G. Dill.
F. Anet.
S. Eneldo.
D. Dil.

PARTS USED
The Leaves and Seeds.

PREPARATION.
An Oil by Infusion &c.

PLACE.
Gardens only.

TIME.
It Flowers and Ripens the seed. in July and Augus.

DESCRIPTION.

The Stalks 1 are Craneld, of a dark, rather then light Green. The Leaves 2, are something like Fennel, but flatter in the Branches. The Flower. 3, Grow in Umbles on the top of the Stalks, having Each five Curld round Leaves (And grow on the tops of the Seeds) encircling five Yellow Chives, with Summits and Farina the same. In the Centre is a Short Yellowish Green Style. The Seed 4, is Rib'd, of a Dark Brown, edged round with a very light Brown, Convex on one side and on the other Concave. 5 is one Part of the Umble, and 6 Shews the bottom part of the Leaf that clasp round the Stalk.

Timothy Sheldrake, 'Dill' (*Anethum graveolens*), from *Botanicum Medicinale* (1756–9).

'It is in vain to describe an herb so commonly known', wrote Culpeper.[25] He felt the same about wild thyme (mother of thyme), *T. serpyllum* – and included no culinary information about either. In fact he had little to say about the culinary uses of the herbs he described, and said that chervil 'is sown in gardens for a sallad herb'.

Culpeper thought that dill, compared with fennel, had 'a strong unpleasant scent'.[26] He also believed that 'cives' (chives, *Allium schoenoprasum*) were dangerous unless administered by a physician. He wrote,

Chive blossom (*Allium schoeno-prasum*). These edible blossoms make wonderful garnishes.

if they be eaten raw (I do not mean raw, opposite to roasted or boiled, but raw, opposite to chymical preparation) they send up very hurtful vapours to the brain, causing troublesome sleep, and spoiling the eye-sight, yet of them prepared by the art of the alchymist, may be made an excellent remedy for the stoppage of the urine.[27]

Culpeper tells us that watercress (*Nasturtium officinalis*) 'tastes somewhat hot and sharp'. He also advises 'those that would live in health, may use it if they please; if they will not, I cannot help it. If any fancy not pottage, they may eat the herb as a sallad.'[28] The familiar flowers called 'nasturtiums' (*Tropaeolum majus*) are in the same family, and produce similar pungency in varying degrees. 'Cress' refers to three different

The nasturtium's (*Tropaeolum majus*) flowers and leaves add a hot, mustard-like kick to salads and sandwiches.

plants: upland cress, *Barbarea verna*, watercress and garden cress, *Lepidium sativum*. They all share a peppery taste due to the presence of compounds in common with other cruciferous species, such as horseradish and mustard.

Less Common Herbs

A great number of herbs that were once well known are less familiar today, and tend to be overlooked except by gardeners or serious cooks who are always searching for unusual ingredients. Occasionally, they are rediscovered and enjoy a resurgence of popularity; rocket (arugula) and coriander (cilantro) are typical. Pliny believed that rocket (*Eruca vesicaria* subs. *sativa*) was 'a great provocative of lust' and recommended that it be combined with lettuce, so that 'the excess of cold in the one [be] compensated by the equal degree of heat in the other'.[29] Culpeper thought rocket was only of use as a 'sallad herb', hence not worthy of mention. He does opine at length about 'common wild rocket', with description and medical usage. Rocket – the Egyptians called it *ethrekigkin* – has been a popular salad green in Europe for ages but was rediscovered in American kitchens only in the past decade or so. Culpeper also thought angelica (*Angelica archangelica*) was 'so well known to be growing almost in every garden', yet today it is only known, if at all, for its pale green candied stems.[30]

Calamus or sweet flag (*Acorus calamus*) was familiar to the ancient Egyptians, who used it medicinally, and as an aphrodisiac. Today its essential oil is an ingredient in some teas and liqueurs: Altvater, Benedictine, Campari, some gins, vermouth and both yellow and green Chartreuse. Egyptians knew chamomile (*Chamaemelum nobile*), but we don't know what use they made of it. Culpeper, once again, considered the plant to be too familiar to merit a description, let alone mention its culinary properties (all the teas, decoctions, infusions in wine and so on, according to that herbalist, served medical purposes only). He felt the same way about lavender (*Lavandula* spp.) – which was indeed well known, and had been for a long time – the lavender used in Ancient Egypt (*L. stoechas*) was called *suphlo*.

Gardeners know several *Achillea* species, such as iva (*A. moschata*) and yarrow (*A. millefolium*), but are probably unaware that the astringent, bitter and peppery foliage has been used sparingly to flavour cheeses, in place of hops in some beers and as a bitter component in various *digestifs*. Another component of *digestifs* is balm, or lemon balm. Native to southern Europe, it could be grown in medieval monastery gardens well into the more temperate zones. Monks used it in their formularies for liqueurs, such as Benedictine (which is actually a fairly modern recipe in the style of the drinks invented by monks) and Chartreuse. Its use probably diminished when inexpensive lemons from warmer climates became available in the twentieth century. Today it is finding renewed popularity precisely because its lemony scent is milder, and it doesn't have the same intensely acidic taste – it's like a Meyer lemon in herbal form. Another lemon substitute from ancient times was verbena. Hippocrates, in his *Materia Medica*, lists verbena (*Verbena officinalis*), but it's not the one we know today. Ours (*Aloysia triphylla*) is from South America and could not have been known in pre-Columbian Rome. Both species get their lemony aroma from the same compound: citral.

Of course, the herb we most associate with beer is hops (*Humulus lupulus*) – the bitter compound lupulin acts as a preservative. Ancient Babylon's Jews flavoured their barley beer with hops. Pliny the Elder described young shoots of hops cooked as a pot-herb. It was mentioned by Hildegard, the Abbess of Rupertsburg, as an additive for oat beer, in 1097, and was used in Holland from the early fourteenth century.[31] Supposedly, 'herisie and beere came hopping into England both in a yeere' – as Henry Buttes wrote in 1599 (*Dyet's Dry Dinner*). The 'yeere' in question was 1524, when the Lollards were stirring up dissent against the Roman Catholic Church

Lavender (*Lavandula angustifolia*), a cultivar named 'Hidecote', in Cornell University's herb garden.

Leonhart Fuchs,
'Hops' (*Humulus
lupulus*), from *De
Historia Stirpium*
(1549), engraving.

(well before Henry VIII decided that excommunication was
preferable to an heirless marriage). Buttes was mistaken about
hops, though – they had been in England since Roman times.
In fact, England's Henry IV banned the use of hops in beer
in the early fifteenth century. That prohibition was dropped
during the reign of Edward VI, a century and a half later.

Marijuana (*Cannabis sativa*) was used in place of hops in
the beer known as 'Hi-Brew'; no longer produced, it was made
in Amsterdam by Brouwerij 't IJ. Obviously a popular intox-
icant on its own, marijuana – sometimes casually referred to
as 'herb' on the street – actually has had some use, historically,
as a culinary herb. Mapouchari is a kind of compound butter
made with marijuana in Egypt. The seeds were fried in ancient
Scythia as a dessert. Marijuana seeds, *asanomi*, are used in Japanese tofu 'burgers', called *ganmo*. In Eastern Europe, especially
Poland and Russia, the seeds are parched and eaten. Like Alice
B. Toklas's famous 'brownies' – which were actually fudge –

A moeos. Crisantemis uocant egyp
tij: hym. Romani: tantum uocat.
Alij: tana citam. Alij: tanacipan.
Vna cura es siquis febribus uocat.
erbe artemesie tagantes sine
cum cum oleo roseo pungε.
febres statim tollit. Ad uesice dolo
erbe arteme rem istrangui
sie tagantes. ex sueo riam,
scriptula duo. rum cyatum unu.
dabis bibere. si febricitanta. febri
citantiu. maqua calida cyathos
duos. et remedium erit. Ad cogna
erbam artemetum dolorem.
siam tagantum tundis cum
axungia. ra ceto. subigis. ponis.
ligabis. tera die sine aliqua dis
ficultate sanabit. Ad neruoap do
erbam artemesi lorem ··
am tagantem cum oleo be
ne subactam imponis. mirifice
sanat. A pedum dolorem siquis g
erbe arteme iur ugiatur,
sie radicem cum melle dabis
manducare. pt cenam. liberabi
tur. ur iur credi possit. tantum
bre uirturem. Si infante hilare
erbam artemesi sanat.
am incende. r subfumigabis
infantem. onis incursiones auer
tat. Nom istur hebet. Artemesia.
leptasilos uirtutes plures haber

erba ista nascit circa fossas. ut
cea sepes. uf aggeres. flores es. ut
folia ipsius. si conriueris: sambuc
odorem hnt. Ad stomachi dolorem
erbam artemesiam leptafillu
tunsam cum oleo amigdalino be
ne subactam more malagmatis. inon
cis in panno mundo. linies. quinto die
sanabit. rsi siut es arcemesie radix su
plum edificu suspensa: domui nemo
nocebit.

erbe arteme. Ad neruoap dolore.
sie leptafillis suetum cum oleo
wsario mixtum: pungis eos. desinit
dolor. ex tumor. roisie uitium tollit.
Nam has tres artemesias: diana dies
inuenisse. uirtutes earti. r medicari
ta. chirom centauro tradidit. q pmi
de his herbis medicinam instruit.
has autem herbas. ex nomine diane.

This French poster advertises Absinthe de Pontarlier, 19th century.

hashish is made into candy (*majoun*) in Algeria and Morocco. It is made of dried fruits such as dates, figs and raisins, and seasoned with aniseed, cinnamon, ginger, honey and ground almonds or walnuts. Few of the ancients ever thought of smoking this herb, though the Assyrians did sometimes burn it – 'in fumigation to dispel sorrow or grief'.[32]

Mugwort (*Artemisia vulgaris*) and wormwood (*A. absinthium*) both appear in Hippocrates' *Materia Medica*. Artemisias were known in antiquity: the Romans believed that the goddess Diana first gave them to Chiron, the Centaur who instructed Aesculapius in the art of medicine. We know wormwood today as the key ingredient in absinthe, and Pliny described a wormwood-flavoured wine called *absintites*. Tansy (*Tanacetum vulgare*) is another bitter, aromatic and vaguely citrusy herb that is reminiscent of absinthe.

Horehound's (*Marrubium vulgare*) generic name is derived from Hebrew '*marob*', and it was originally one of the seder's

Horehound (*Marrubium vulgare*) in the herb gardens of Cornell University, New York City.

bitter herbs. To temper its bitterness the herb was often combined with honey (for example, to reduce respiratory problems). Today, that usage survives – just barely – in old-fashioned cough drops (horehound syrups for this purpose were common in Culpeper's day). Craig Claiborne, writing in 1963, listed horehound among the 'herbs and spices with limited, quaint, or questionable virtues', describing candy made from it as 'rather unpleasant [and] perverse-tasting', but there are still a few of us who disagree.[33]

The names of some herbs have survived from ancient times but they may no longer be applied to the same plants today. The 'hyssop' mentioned in the Bible is not the modern hyssop, *Hyssopus officinalis*, but probably one of the many herbs known today as 'za'atar'. According to chemists Alexander Fleisher and Zhenia Fleisher, who specialize in the study of the kinds of aromatic oils found in herbs, the most likely species to have been the biblical hyssop is *Majorana syriaca*.[34] Za'atar is a collective name for a group of herbs used in the Middle East. It includes members of several genera (*Calamintha*, *Origanum*, *Satureja* and *Thymus*). What they have in common is a high concentration of thymol, the essential oil characteristic of thyme and for which it is named. The herb should not be confused with a spice blend also called *zathar* and *zattar* that is popular in the region: it is usually a ground mixture of dried thyme (or za'atar), toasted sesame seeds and sumac berries. The herb and the seasoning mixture are mixed with olive oil as a dip for bread.

Another plant that is commonly used to add a tart, sour taste to foods in what was once known as 'the Levant' – but is rarely utilized elsewhere – is sumac (*Rhus pentaphylla* and *R. tripartite*), species indigenous to the Mediterranean basin. Their flavour is reminiscent of green apples because of their malic acid content (*Malus* being the genus for apples). Sumac is featured in Arabic, Kurdish, Persian and Turkish dishes. The New World's equivalents are smooth sumac (*R. glabra*) and staghorn sumac (*R. typhina*). They can be used the same ways as their Old World cousins, but – as Boy Scouts can tell you – they are easily made into a tart, lemonade-like beverage. Any *Rhus* species that has white berries should never be touched – they are best known as poison ivy (*R. toxicodendron*), poison oak (*R. diversiloba*) and poison sumac (*R. vernix*).

Other herbs, once very popular, have virtually disappeared from our kitchens. Lovage is one of the most-often included herbs in Apicius' *De Re Coquinaria* (along with rue), yet is rarely seen except on menus that consciously try to recreate the flavour of long-lost dishes. It has a strong celery-like aroma. Dioscorides tells us that the Egyptians knew rue (*Ruta graveolens*) as *ephnoubon*. Hippocrates' *Materia Medica* listed the herb. Exceedingly bitter, rue was nonetheless a popular ingredient in Ancient Rome, and Pliny says it was added to honeyed wine in the third century BCE.

One herb that has a well-known but very narrow usage is woodruff (*Galium odoratum*). This native of the Mediterranean region is known primarily for its use in flavouring May wine or Maiwein, a popular spring drink in Germany now made commercially with artificial flavouring, since woodruff is toxic in all but small amounts.

An entire group of plants have been developed solely for their scents: geraniums (*Pelargonium* spp.) come in a wide range of scented species and have been bred to produce dozens of scented cultivars and hybrids, such as apple geranium (*P. odoratissimum*), chocolate mint geranium (*P. tomentosum*), lemon geranium (*P. crispum*) and nutmeg geranium (*P. fragrans*).

Some wild herbs went on to become carefully cultivated plants. Queen Anne's lace (*Daucus carota*) is the weedy ancestor of the subspecies *D. carota* L. ssp. *sativus* – our domestic carrot.

Rue (*Ruta graveolens* 'Blue Mound'), another bitter herb.

Though the roots are too tough to eat, the foliage makes a flavourful addition to soups, and the seeds have a warm caraway-like taste. The common name refers to the beheading of Henry VIII's second wife Anne Boleyn, who wore a large lacy collar to her execution. In the exact centre of each flower, there's a tiny dot of deep bloody red.

There are some wild herbs that are never intentionally planted anymore – stinging nettles (*Urtica dioica*), for example. The botanical name is derived from the Latin for 'I burn.' If handled carefully, with heavy gloves and long sleeves, the leaves make an excellent pot-herb or soup green in early spring. The tiny stinging needles are rendered harmless by the heat of cooking. Samuel Pepys mentioned 'some nettle porridge' that he enjoyed on 25 February 1661.[35] The nettles' sting, by the way, is caused by formic acid in tiny needle-like hairs on the leaves and stems. It's the same compound that causes the burning sensation of ant bites.

Salad herbs were used as such long before John Evelyn published his pamphlet, *Acetaria: A Discourse of Sallets*, in 1699. Pot-herbs have also been in use, at least since early man discovered how to use fire to prepare food. Today we tend to think of 'herbs' as another form of spice, a seasoning for other foods, rather than as foods in their own right. It has not always been so (and, as we will see elsewhere, this broader sense of herbs is still in force in some parts of the world). Theophrastus called purslane (*Portulaca oleracea*) '*andrákhne*', and mentioned its use as a cooked green. Culpeper thought its use as a 'sallad herb' too well-known to require mention. It is still occasionally eaten as a salad green and pot-herb today. The sour young greens of sorrel (*Rumex* spp.) are cooked in soups. Oxalic acid provides the sharp tang, which becomes more pronounced as the plant matures. The acid is said to soften the bones of fish – so it is often cooked with pike (which has free-floating forked bones that are difficult to remove) – although it is unlikely that the minute quantities of oxalic acid would have much effect on those deeply embedded bones. Watercress (*Nasturtium officinale*) is pleasantly pungent; the name of the genus is derived from the Latin words for 'twist the nose'. Pliny recommended that a 'sluggish man should eat nasturtium, to arouse him from his torpidity'.[36] The edible flowers we call 'nasturtiums' are a different species (*Tropaeolum majus*) but contain the same peppery compound, phenylethylene isothiocyanate, that gives wasabi and mustard their bite. Those 'nasturtiums' originated in the Andes of South America, so would never have been known to Pliny.

Bergamots (*Monarda* spp.) are usually grown for their flowers, but the flowers and foliage contain thymol – the principle flavour component of thyme – and can be used in place of that herb, or brewed into tea. They should not be confused, however, with the bergamot in Earl Gray tea. *That* 'bergamot' is actually a kind of bitter orange (*Citrus aurantium* subs. *Bergamia*) whose dried peels are used in formulating many distilled beverages, such as Altvater, Amaretto, gin and Grand Marnier.

Borage (*Borago officinalis*), little-known today, was – according to Culpeper –

> chiefly used as a cordial, and [is] good for those that are weak in long sickness, and to comfort the heart and spirits of those that are in a consumption, or troubled with often swoonings, or passions of the heart.[37]

Today, cordials still cheer our hearts – but not in the medical sense that Culpeper meant. For example, borage lends its herbal flavour to some alcoholic mixtures (it's reputed to be one of the secret ingredients in Pimm's No. 1); one synonym, 'cool tankard', implies that usage. It has a slight cucumber taste, which is why Pimm's is usually garnished with a slice of cucumber. Burnet (*Poterium sanguisorba*), native to southern Europe, was at one time a common salad herb, as the name 'salad burnet' suggests. Like borage it has a cucumber-like flavour but its delicate foliage makes it a better garnish than the rather coarse leaves of borage. Cooked borage, however, is a popular filling for many local varieties of Italian ravioli (such as the *agnolotti* of Novara, *mandili 'nversoi* from Piemonte and *zembi d'arzillo* from Liguria) and as a green colourant for spinach-like pastas (*bardele coi morai*, from Lombardy, *corzetti* from Piemonte, *tagliolini* and *picagge* from Liguria, and *stracci* from Ciociaria).

Catnip or catmint (*Nepeta cataria*) was known in the ancient world as a medicinal herb, but was grown as a culinary herb

Catnip (*Nepeta cataria*), because our gardens are not just for the enjoyment of humans.

for use in soups and stews back as far as the fifteenth century. It was still a condiment and an ingredient in sauces in eighteenth-century England. There is some difference of opinions among feline connoisseurs of catnip. Some of our cats have indulged in the drug openly, some furtively, while others seem willing to defend to the death their little stashes from any potential intruders. Most cats prefer the dried herb – no doubt because of its concentrated dose of the active ingredient, nepetalactone – other cats simply lie in the middle of a patch of catnip, grazing in a kind of nepeta-induced stupor.

Pliny the Elder listed chicory and lettuce (*Cichorium intybus* and *Lactuca* spp.) in Book xix of his *Natural History*. Lettuce was also mentioned by Horace and Virgil as a salad herb. He said that it grew wild and was cultivated in Egypt, where it was known as *seris*. He also warned of certain purple forms of Lettuce 'known to some persons as the *astytis*, and to others as the *eunychion*, it having the effect, in a remarkable degree, of quenching the amorous propensities'.[38] That is, they had the opposite effect of aphrodisiacs (we suspect that the demand for such salad ingredients was similarly quenched by that assertion). Radicchio is a variety of chicory that has become a popular salad ingredient, and is sometimes braised as a vegetable. The diminutive Italian name is derived from Latin 'radix', meaning 'root' (a number of bitter Mediterranean greens – such as chicory, dandelions and lettuces – have strong tap roots). The names 'endive' and 'chicory' are derived from the Arabic *hindeb* and *schikhrieh*, respectively. Culpeper doesn't even mention chicory. The young leaves of dandelion (*Taraxacum officinale* ssp. *officinale*) make a pleasant early spring salad, the older foliage a pot-herb, the dried roots (like those of chicory) can be roasted as a substitute for coffee, and the flowers flavour an old-fashioned wine. Greeks refer to any wild greens as *horta* – amaranth, dandelions, mustard greens, nettles or any other bitter green found growing in the wild; in Mexico, they're *quelites*.

Herb Gardens

According to Pliny, 'Epicurus, that connoisseur in the enjoyments of a life of ease, was the first to lay out a garden at Athens; up to his time it had never been thought of, to dwell in the country in the middle of the town.'[39] The gardens Pliny described were vegetable and flower gardens, but both contained herbs. Herb gardens as we know them began to appear in the late Middle Ages, coinciding with the rise in popularity of herbal books. Other classical writers whose work influenced the design of medieval and Renaissance herb gardens include Cato (*De Agri Cultura*), Columella (*De Re Rustica*), Dioscorides (*De Materia Medica*), Palladius (*Opus Agriculturae* or *De Re Rustica*) and Varro (*Rerum Rusticarum*).

Around 795, Charlemagne issued a charter that specified how everything in his empire (the Holy Roman Empire) was to be managed. The seventieth chapter of his *Capitulare de villis vel curtis imperialibus* (*Charter of Imperial Lands and Imperial Courts*) included a listing of all the plants he required to be grown in his gardens throughout the empire. The culinary herbs included *abrotanum* (southernwood, *Artemisia abrotanum*), *adripias* (garden orache, *Atriplex hortensis*), *ameum* (spignel, *Meum athamanticum*), *anesum* (aniseed, *Pimpinella anisum*), *anetum* (dill), *cerfolium* (chervil), *ciminum* (cumin, *Cuminum cyminum*), *coriandrum* (coriander), *costum* (costmary, *Tanacetum balsamita*), *diptamnum* (dittany of Crete, *Origanum dictamnus*), *febrefugiam* (common centaury, *Centaurium erythrae*), *fenicolum* (fennel), *fenigrecum* (fenugreek, *Trigonella foenum-graecum*), *intubas* (chicory), *levisticum* (lovage), *malvas* (mallows), *mentam* (wild mint, *Mentha arvensis*),

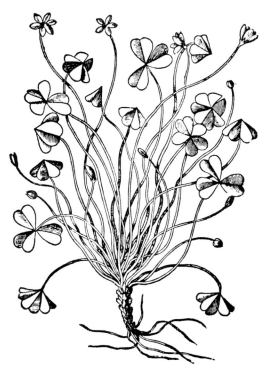

P. A. Mattioli (trans.), (*Oxalis* spp.), *Les commentaries sur les six livres de la matiere medecinale de Pedacius Dioscuride* (1565), engraving.

mentastrum (apple mint, *M. suaveolens*), *nastursium* (garden cress), *neptam népite* (catnip), *olisatum* (alexanders, *Smyrnium olustrum*), *parduna* (burdock, *Arctium lappa*), *peledium* (pennyroyal), *petresilinum* (parsley), *rosmarinum* (rosemary), *rutam* (rue), *salviam* (sage), *satureium* (savory), *sclareiam* (clary sage, *Salvia sclarea*), *sinape* (mustard), *sisimbrium* (water mint, *M. aquatica*), *tanazitam* (tansy), and *vulgigina* (European wild ginger, *Asarum europaeum*). Charlemagne's requirements for gardens, laid out in clean grids, would have included many other medicinal and practical herbs (such as madder, *Rubia tinctorum*).[40]

In the ninth century a plan was developed (but never executed) for a Swiss Benedictine monastery at St Gall. The

Apuleius Platonicus, 'Rhizotomists Gathering Herbs', from *Herbarium*, *c.* 1200.

Hieronymus Brunschwig, 'A Medieval Garden of Herbs', from *Liber de Arte Distillandi* (1500), engraving.

plan includes kitchen and medicinal gardens, *herbers* – neat raised beds in the former for chervil, coriander, dill, lettuce, parsley and savory; the latter to be planted with lovage, pennyroyal, peppermint, rue, sage, savory and watercress. At the end of the thirteenth century Albertus Magnus recommended borders of fragrant herbs, where 'men may sit down there to take their repose pleasurably when their senses need refreshment'.[41] A fifteenth-century illustration of a herb garden appears in Piero de' Crescendi's *Liber Ruralium Commodorum*, a guidebook for managing country estates. Such estates were thought to be safe from the ills of the cities, including the plague. Boccaccio's *Decameron* is set on just such an estate, outside of Florence. In fact, many gardens of the period were based on descriptions in the *Decameron*. Such gardens were highly stylized recreations of the nature that was already disappearing in Europe, small representations of paradise lost; indeed, the plan for St Gall used the term *paradise* for the gardens that provided cut flowers for the church.

In the Renaissance the efficient grids and raised beds gave way to more ornamental layouts. In particular, knotted and more complex geometric patterns – often with carefully chosen coloured gravel between the beds, and bordered by perfectly pruned hedges of boxwood or rosemary – began to be seen (in England, during the reign of Elizabeth I). Good examples of knot gardens can be seen, today, at Antony House (Cornwall), Hatfield House (Hertfordshire), St Fagans (South Wales), Knowle (Solihull) and Red Lodge Museum (Bristol), in the UK; Alexandra Hicks Herb Knot Garden (University of Michigan), the Brooklyn Botanical Gardens and the Cleveland Botanical Garden (Ohio) in the USA; and Anzac Square, Dunedin, New Zealand.

A cartouche from the title page of some editions of Gerard's *Herball* (1597) showing simple rectangular raised beds.

A walled garden would be known as *Hortus Conclusus*. Boccaccio's *Decameron* described an Italian walled garden in the mid-fifteenth century. Such gardens often exhibited ancient sculpture (or copies thereof) or fragments of ruins – a foreshadowing of the follies and *fabriques* that began to built on English and French estates in the eighteenth century. Some design elements were borrowed from Moorish sources, at the same time as Western Europeans were rediscovering the classic literature, philosophy and science that had been preserved in Islamic libraries. Some Islamic gardens, such as the one in Spain's Alhambra, featured sunken beds, arranged in Roman-style grids, to facilitate watering in the dry climate.

John Parkinson,
Paradisi in Sole,
Paradisus Terrestris,
1629, engraving.

William Lawson, plan for a knotted garden, from *The Country Housewife's Garden* (1618), engraving.

Some eighteenth-century herb gardens have been preserved (or recreated). Pomona Hall, just outside modern Camden, New Jersey, has brick paths between beds of familiar herbs that would have been brought from Europe: garlic chives, lemon balm, lamb's ears (*Stachys* spp.), lavender, lovage, mint, rosemary, sage, thyme and yarrow.

Following the Age of Exploration and the rise of colonialism, herb gardens began to incorporate more exotic species brought back from the far ends of empire. The Victorians, especially, loved to fill their homes with large and often bizarre tropical species, such as *Monstera deliciosa* and various palms.

Isabelle Forrest, 'An Edwardian herb border in June', watercolour. Left, back to front: caraway, tarragon, rue, mint, parsley, sage, thyme, purple sage, chives and thyme. Right, back to front: lemon balm, sorrel, borage, chamomile, alkanet (*Anchusa officinalis*, also known as dyer's bugloss) and pot marigold.

Such decorations paralleled the trophy heads of exotic animals upon Victorian walls – both celebrated British supremacy at a time when its Empire had reached its greatest extent.

Later still, Victorian excesses were rejected in favour of older styles. Medieval and Renaissance styles began to re-emerge, and the gardens at Sissinghurst and Long Barn (created in the period between 1927 and 1954 by Vita Sackville-West) combine their structures with a more modern appreciation of contrasts between plants of varying colour and texture. Sackville-West had no interest in cooking – the only time she kept the herb garden near the kitchen was during the food shortages of the Second World War – but her decorative herb gardens featured plenty of culinary herbs. Long Barn's gardens included basil, bergamot, chicory, hyssop, sage, at least two lavenders, two marjorams (including a pink variety), peppermint, rue, southernwood, sweet cicely (*Myrrhis odorata*), sweet woodruff, tarragon,

Peter Schoeffer, 'Violet' (*Viola spp.*), from *Der Gart der Gesundheit* (1485), engraving.

thymes and verbena. Sissinghurst's garden was even more extensive, adding two sages, three bergamots, five mints, seven types of thyme and many more unusual species, such as calamint (*Calamintha nepeta*), good King Henry (*Chenopodium bonus-henricus*), horehound, melitot (*Mellitotus officinalis*), plus old lady (*Artemisia maritima*) and old man (southernwood).

Sackville-West was influenced, as were many other people, by the work of Eleanour Sinclair Rohde, a designer of, and a writer about, gardening. Her books on herbs include *A Garden of Herbs* (1920), *The Old-World Pleasaunce* (1925), *Herbs and Herb Gardening* (1936) and *Culinary and Salad Herbs* (1940). In *The Old English Herbals* (1922), she wrote:

> books on herbs were studied in England as early as the eighth century . . . we know that Boniface, 'the Apostle of the Saxons,' received letters from England asking him for books on simples and complaining that it was difficult to obtain the foreign herbs mentioned in those we already possessed. But of these manuscripts none have survived, the oldest we possess being of the tenth century.[42]

One of the earliest English books on herbs was a Saxon translation of the *Herbarium Apuleii Platonici*.

Rohde may have been responsible for a modern rebirth of interest in herb gardening in England and elsewhere. However, as she has shown, it is clear that the English have been interested in herbs for a very long time. Time and space may limit many modern herb gardeners to a few pots on a sunny windowsill, but the tradition continues nonetheless.

3
A Less Eurocentric Herbarium

Africa, Asia, Australia and the Americas have their own herbs, quite different from the usual suspects. Some are from families of plants that are not found in Europe. Some have not yet found a European market demand large enough to justify their export (this may change, as the insatiable craving for culinary novelty drives international trade). Many of these exotic species are used in similar fashion to their European counterparts, but sometimes they are so different from European cuisine that they nearly constitute completely new forms of cookery.

Africa

African cooks tend to use spice mixtures more than herbs as seasoning (and, considering Africa's history, they tend to be European or Arabic in nature). Most of the herbs used in African cookery are native to Europe and the Americas (curry leaf, *Murraya koenigii*; Kaffir lime leaf, *Citrus hystrix*; and lemongrass, *Cymbopogon citrates*, are Asian exceptions). Indigenous herbs are often used as pot-herbs, in sauces or in brewing teas, rather than as seasoning.

Pot-herbs are leafy vegetables that tend to be cooked in stews, soups or braised dishes, all moist cooking methods. *Efo* is the generic African term for edible green leaves, much like the Mexican *quelites*. One of the main uses of such plants is as a thickener for liquid foods. Baobab (*Adansonia digitata*), as an example, is used as a foodstuff only in West Africa, even though the trees are common in Eastern and Southern Africa. The leaves are eaten as cooked greens and as additions to condiments, relishes, soups and stews. They thicken these moist dishes, much as okra does, and such sauces make a welcome addition to starchy staple foods. For example: *danwake* is a Hausa dish of cassava, chillis, black-eyed beans (peas), sorghum and sweet potatoes, cooked in peanut oil, and bound with a sauce thickened by baobab leaves.[1]

Ebolo (*Crassocephalum crepidioides*) or in Sierra Leone, *bologi*, grows in West Africa, where the leaves and young shoots are prepared as pot-herbs. Lagos *bologi* is a different plant, used in similar fashion; it is actually waterleaf (*Talinum fruticosum*). Similarly, the young foliage of *soko* (*Celosia argentea*), a plant that is closely related to amaranth, provides a pot-herb in Benin, Congo and Nigeria, where it is cooked in *dende* (red palm oil), with aubergine (eggplant), chillis and onions, along with fish or meat.[2] In Nigeria the Yoruban name *sokoyokoto*

> literally means 'the vegetable that makes your husband's face rosy,' which we think is a wry – maybe sly – joke shared among women in the marketplace.[3]

Other wild herbs used as pot-herbs in Africa include beggar ticks (*Bidens pilosa*) or Spanish needle, which are native to South America but are weeds throughout much of the world. Even though the young leaves are eaten as pot-herbs in central and western Africa, it's considered a noxious weed in eastern Africa. The young foliage of moringa (*Moringa oleifera* and twelve other *Moringa* species) is cooked like spinach and its roots are grated as a substitute for horseradish.

Egusi is a thick soup that is popular all over West Africa. It is often thickened with seeds from various watermelon-like plants, such as fluted pumpkin (*Telfairia occidentalis*). The leaves and shoots of fluted pumpkin, known as *ugu* leaf, are used as pot-herbs all over West Africa. Louisiana gumbo, thickened with filé powder, made from ground leaves and cambium (inner bark) of sassafras (*Sassafras albidum*) was originally an African slaves' substitute for *egusi*. Mulukhiyyah (bush okra, comfrey – not to be confused with the European medicinal herb *Symphytum peregrinum* – jew's marrow, nalta jute, *Corchorus olitorius*) is available dried, fresh or frozen. Fresh leaves provide mucilaginous thickening to soups and stews, as true okra serves in gumbos – and, like okra, if allowed to boil it becomes unpleasantly stringy and gummy. This Middle Eastern ingredient is found throughout Muslim-influenced Africa, especially Egypt – but is also popular in Japan and the Philippines, where it's known as *saluyot*. There is another plant called mulukhiyyah, an unrelated species not yet identified, that is used in Morocco (also as a thickener). Its pods are used, rather than its foliage, making it more like okra – the name and usage were applied in Morocco, perhaps by pilgrims returning from Mecca who had encountered *C. olitorius* in the east. The same, or similar, plant is known in India as *mitha pakh*.

In African cookery it is sometimes difficult to decide whether a dish is a soup, a stew or a sauce. 'Soup-sauce-stew' is more of a continuum than separate categories. Several different plants provide the viscosity that, in classic French cuisine, is found in emulsion-based sauces such as beurre blanc, hollandaise and mayonnaise, and starch-thickened sauces like velouté and béchamel.

The dried and powdered leaves of the baobab tree are known as *kuka*, and *kadaro* is a viscous sauce made from kuka. *Tibati* is a similar sauce served with beans. Sauces and stews called 'palaver sauce', are thickened with cassava (*Manihot esculenta*) leaves in the West African countries of Ghana, Liberia, Nigeria and Sierra Leone. A similar dish, *pondu*, is made in the Democratic Republic of the Congo. Cassava is native to the Brazilian rainforest, where it is primarily consumed as a root vegetable. It is eaten that way in Africa as well (sub-Saharan Africans obtain more of their nutrition from roots and tubers than the inhabitants of any other place in the world).

Some African herbs are treated not just as pot-herbs, but as salad herbs. The leaves and flowers of tasselflowers (*Emilia coccinea* and *E. sonchifolia*), for example, are eaten both ways. They are indigenous to tropical Asia but commonly grown in Ghana. Bananas (*Musa* spp.) are native to Africa, where they are most commonly eaten as fruit but the leaves and flowers are also used in cooking – in salads, as pot-herbs and, especially the leaves, as food wrappers (though such uses are much more common in south Asia and Mexico than in Africa). Yanrin or wild lettuce (*Launaea taraxacifolia,* sometimes listed as *Sonchus taraxacifolius*) is native to Ethiopia, but grows wild in disturbed African soils between the Equator and the Tropic of Cancer, as well as in Tanzania. In Nigeria cultivated versions are preferred – they're less bitter than the wild plants. Young leaves are cooked in soups and added to salads.

Herbal teas, infusions or tisanes are commonly brewed from herbs in Africa and, as in Europe and elsewhere, they blur the lines between social beverages and medicines. Khat (*Catha edulis*) grows as a small evergreen tree in Ethiopia, Somalia, Yemen and Zambia. Its leaves are brewed as tea. Its stimulating effect is due to the presence of cathinone – an amphetamine-like drug – and the milder cathine. The concentration of cathinone is highest in fresh leaves. While it is legal in some Middle Eastern countries – Israel, Oman and Yemen – it is illegal in Canada and the UK, and listed as a Schedule 1 Controlled Substance in the USA.

Not criminal, but linked – botanically – to one of the most famous herbs said to possess psychoactive properties, African

Of wormwode.

 Blinthium is named in greke Apsinthion, because no beast will touch it for bitternes, & in English wormwode, because it killeth wormes, I suppose that it was ones called worme crout, for in some part of Fresland (from whence semeth a great part of our englysh tonge to haue come) it is so called euen vnto this daye: in Duche wermut, in frenche aluine or absence.

VVormvuode Romane.   Absinthium Ponticum Romæ natum.

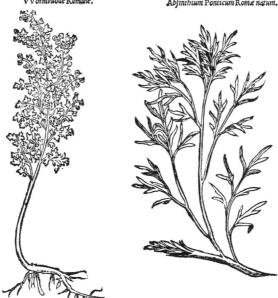

William Turner, 'Wormwood' (*Artemisia spp.*) from *A New Herball* (1551), engraving.

wormwood (*Artemisia afra*) is known as *wilde-als* in South Africa (in Afrikaans) and *zengana* in Southern Sotho. Elsewhere, it's *umhlonyane* in Xhosa, *mhlonyane* in Zulu and *lengana* in Tswan. This bitter relative of the European plant that gives us absinthe is sometimes brewed as a tisane, or tea. Indigenous to South Africa, it grows wild all the way to Ethiopia – it's the African equivalent of the sagebrush (*A. tridentata*) that grows in the American west.

Mulukhiyyah's dried leaves are sometimes also brewed as a herbal tea. Presumably the herb loses its mucilaginous properties when dried.

Honeybush leaves (*Cyclopia genistoides*, *C. intermedia*, *C. sessiliflora*, *C. subternata*) are chopped, moistened and left to ferment. They are then dried, much as black tea (*Camellia sinensis*) is, but the resulting herbal tea has no caffeine and little tannin. It is beginning to become popular with tea-drinkers outside Africa. The best-known African herbal tea, however, is rooibos (red bush, *Aspalathus linearis*). Its leaves are also moistened and dried and oxidation produces the tea's reddish-brown colouration. In South Africa rooibos is sometimes brewed so strong that it is considered a variation on espresso. Rooibos, once gathered by Bushmen and Khoikhoi in South Africa, was introduced to the West as a tea substitute that contained no caffeine. It was marketed as *Kaffree*. Today, dozens of brands include rooibos. In the opposite direction – both chemically and geographically – caffeine-laden guarana (*Paullinia cupana*), from South America, is featured in a number of commercial 'energy drinks'. Despite its name, rooibos is not the reddest herbal tea on the continent – wild rosella's (*Hibiscus sabdariffa*) flowers add flavour and lend a lovely red colour to cool drinks, like the *bissap* or *zobo* of Ghana and Nigeria, and teas throughout Africa.

A few African herbs are used primarily as *seasoning*, much as in traditional European cooking. Tea-bush (*Ocimum gratissimum*) – which, ironically, is not brewed as tea – and partminger (known as curry leaf in Nigeria, *O. canum*) are popular members of the *Lamiaceae* family. Familiar European *Lamiaceae* herbs include marjoram, oregano, rosemary, sage and thyme, most of which are also used in Nigeria. No one looks for these cousins of basil in the market, since they can be easily grown from seed, or just gathered as weeds. Their fresh leaves season pepper soups in the Delta, where they also serve as pot-herbs; they add a pungent resinous note to *egusi* soups in Kwara; elsewhere they appear raw as a salad.

Lemongrass (*Cymbopogon citrates*) is also known as *koko oba* in Yoruba, *achara ehi* and *akwukuo* in Ibo, *ikonti* in Efik and *myoyaka* in Ibibio. It flavours tea, pepper soups and cooked greens. Fenugreek leaves, dried, are sometimes included in recipes for *berberé* paste, an Ethiopian spice mixture used in cooking and as a condiment. The leaves of doussie (*Afzelia bella*), or papao, are fermented for use as a seasoning for yams. They are called *ule ule* in Ibo.

Bitter-Olubu leaf (Bitter leaf, *Vernonia amygdalina*) is also known as *Etidot* in Cross River State of Nigeria, and *Oriwo* in Benin. Elsewhere in Africa, it's *Ewuro* in Yoruba; *Olubu* or *Onubu* in Ibo. In temperate zones we tend to think of the family *Asteraceae* (formerly *Compositae*) as consisting only of annual or perennial herbs, but in tropical Africa Olubu leaf grows into a 2-metre-tall shrub. The leaves, sold fresh or dried, have a bittersweet quality that is apparent in the stew-like *ndole* cooked in Cameroon, and adds an astringent note to the usual *egusi*. It replaces hops as a bittering agent when making beer in Nigeria. Related species used in similar fashion include *Vernonia calvoana* and *V. colorata*. Utazi-zi *(Crongronema ratifolia)* is used in Nigeria much as the various *Vernonia* species.

Purple basil (*Ocimum basilicum* 'Spicy Globe') can be steeped to make a
deep violet clove-scented herbal vinegar.

Gesho (African dogwood, *Rhamnus prinoides*) is known as *liNyenye* in Swaziland or *mofifi* in South Sotho. It's *blinkblaar* to speakers of Afrikaans, *umGlindi* in Xosa, *umGilindi*, *uNyenye* or *umHlinye* in Zulu. Large branches, leaves or small branches of gesho flavour the East African honey wine *tej* – each one responsible for slightly different flavours. The amount of time that the gesho is infused also affects the flavour – and value – of the *tej*.[4] In South Africa the plant is associated with magic; it is believed to improve hunting, offer protection from lightning and prevent the forces of evil from harming crops. Khat is sometimes added as well.

Za'atar (*Origanum cyriacum*) is a Middle Eastern herb that is commonly used in Moroccan cooking and as a seasoning in the olive oil used by Bedouins of North Africa for dipping bread, a tradition that accompanied the spread of Islam from the Middle East.

While the valleys of African rivers (such as the Nile and Congo) were settled and developed agriculturally some 7,000 years ago, little is known about their cuisine. It wasn't until the Egyptians developed hieroglyphics (and an urge to save information about their daily lives for future generations) that we begin to sense a little about what their cooking might have been like. They left no recipes or menus but their portrayals of agricultural methods suggest a rich and varied cuisine. The fact that they had extensive trade with their neighbours (such as the civilizations in Mesopotamia) suggests some culinary diversity. Egyptians were known to have used *ameset* (dill) and *shaw* (coriander/cilantro), as well as mustard, rosemary and wild marjoram.[5] As Egyptian Vizier Kagemni (*a.* 2321–2290 BCE) once said, 'a mouthful of herbs strengthens the heart.'[6]

East African cuisines were formed as a result of indigenous cooking altered by Persian and Indian migrations. In pre-colonial times North African foods were affected by trade with the Berbers, Carthaginians, Ottomans and Phoenicians, while West African food was influenced first by the Arabs and later by European colonists. Some of the semi-liquid foods eaten in this region are thickened with ground nuts such as peanuts or almonds – a technique which is typical of Arabic cooking, and was popular in Europe during the Middle Ages and Renaissance, only to be replaced by starch-thickened and emulsion-based sauces. Central Africa remained mostly traditional, largely unaffected by outside stimuli. Europe and Asia had a major effect on southern Africa and Malaysian immigrants created a unique cuisine in the far south.

The cuisine of the Cape Malays is what used to be called 'creole' but is now thought of as 'fusion' cooking. It incorporates ideas about food from multiple cultures, from the indigenous Khoisan and Dutch colonists, as well as slaves (Bengalis, East Africans and, of course, Indonesians). Typical Cape Malay foods include *bredies* (meat, tomato and vegetable stews), *bobotie* (curried ground meat casseroles) and *sosaties* (grilled kebabs).

Early Arabic geographers from the tenth century to the sixteenth century's Leo Africanus mentioned food in their reports, but not much about the herbs used; they tended to describe the agriculture of grains, production of meats and dairy products, and sometimes vegetables. Among the vegetables there is mention of mulukhiyyah and baobab. The only herb specifically mentioned was *shih*, which the twelfth-century geographer Al-Idrisi believed to be wormwood.[7] Spices, such as clove and pepper, were already familiar when the Arabs first visited.

Asia and the Pacific

Herbal use is not at all homogeneous in this region. In fact the culinary approach to herbs varies so much that a blanket geographic approach is meaningless. For example, compare China with Vietnam, two countries in close proximity, but with vastly different notions of the place of herbs in their cuisines.

Chinese 'herbs' barely exist as seasoning or salad ingredients. Chinese ingredients are often dried, and very few herbs are used as seasoning. Spices and dried fermented products predominate. If a fresh herb is used at all, it appears only as a garnish (a sprig of coriander, some chopped spring onions/scallions or flat-leaved chives). Chinese cooks rarely serve uncooked plant foods – perhaps because of their use of 'night soil' (human waste) as fertilizer for their gardens. Likewise, raw vegetables, meticulously carved into flowers as garnishes, are not considered to *be* food, but decorations *for* food. Chinese herbal medicine, generally outside the discussion in this book, is noteworthy only because its 'herbs' are rarely herbs at all – in fact, their source may not even be botanical. Among the ingredients considered to be 'herbs', are minerals, dried or preserved snakes and other members of the animal kingdom (or parts thereof, such as rhino horn and deer antlers).

Vietnamese cooks, on the other hand, utilize large amounts of herbs in their meals. They have a range of choices, many of which are virtually unknown outside Vietnam, and almost all of which are used fresh. Strong-flavoured herbs are used by the handful at the table. Diners use cool, fresh lettuce leaves as wrappers to contain various cooked foods, adding any number of pungent or fragrant fresh herbs, such as basil and *cang cua*, to their individual taste. The leaves of various herbs are also suited to the Japanese love of wrapping; think of nori or perilla as wrappers for sushi. Similarly, banana leaves

Holy basil (*Ocimum sanctum*), one of three basils used in Thai kitchens.

are used as wrappers for steamed rice dishes in South-east Asia and as serving dishes in India. La lot leaves, wild betel (*Piper sarmentosum*), is closely related to the betel (*P. betle*) that is famously chewed in South Asia. Wild betel leaf, however, is used as a food wrapper, a Vietnamese version of the way grape leaves are used in the Middle East, or simply stir-fried in *bo xao la lot*.

The foods of Vietnam, Thailand and Laos are classic fusion cuisines – the local tropical diet has been repeatedly altered by contacts from other cultures. Chinese, Indian and European colonials have all had their influence. (Vietnamese cuisine is especially eclectic, since it was long a colony of France – and, no doubt, the later American presence is still affecting Vietnamese eating habits.)

Although Chinese kitchens use few herbs, other Asian cuisines do make use of foliage and flowers. The Japanese have an almost religious affection for nature and their food reflects it – garnishes remind them of the beauty and serenity of the natural world. Garnishes are the visual equivalent of herbs used as seasoning, where the plant provides aroma, taste and sometimes colour to enhance a dish. Basil is essential to Thai cuisine – in fact, several different species of the *Ocimum* genus are in regular use there: lime basil, *O. americanum*; Thai basil, *O. citriodorum*; and holy basil, *O. sanctum*. These are in addition to the familiar sweet basil of Western kitchens. It is also one of the table herbs served in Vietnam.

Cumin leaves and stems – not the more familiar seeds – are eaten fresh or used as a garnish in Vietnam. Likewise, *methi*, fenugreek leaves, flavour breads in India, particularly those baked in Gujarat. Methi is included in some curries and *masalas* used in tandoori cooking. The seeds, with their distinctive maple-like scent, are a major component of curry powder. Curry powder is not an Indian spice – it was invented by British colonials in an attempt to recreate the *masalas* (roasted spice mixtures) that are the soul of Indian 'curries'.

The Vietnamese use of herbs at the table is unlike anything in Western cuisine. Handsful of fragrant, sometimes intensely fragrant herbs are tossed into *pho* (the classic noodle soup of Vietnam), or rolled into lettuce leaves, the Asian equivalent of burritos. Several kinds of basil might be used, along with, or instead of, *cang cua* (*Peperomia pellucida*) – a Vietnamese herb sometimes called 'fish mint' because it smells like mint that has been used to line a fish basket. Another 'fish mint', *giap ca* (*Houttuynia cordata*), is sour, and smells like

Philippe de Noir (printer), title page from *Le Jardin de Sante* (1539), engraving.

fishy coriander. It is rarely used outside Vietnamese dishes, although there is said to be a Japanese version that smells more like oranges. Both are rather peculiar herbs, by Western standards – definitely acquired tastes for non-Vietnamese diners. *Kinh gioi* (*Elsholtzia ciliata*) is more accessible; it's a lemony herb used raw or in cooked Vietnamese dishes. Perilla (*Perilla frutescens*) is also one of the raw herbs on Vietnamese tables, where it is known as *rau tio to*; it tastes like coriander, with hints of cinnamon, lemon and mint. It comes in two basic forms, a fairly smooth green leaf and a ruffled deep red leaf. Both are commonly used in Asian cuisines (the Japanese use both colours in sushi and use the red form to add colour to *umeboshi*, the tiny salted 'plums', and preserved ginger). In Japan perilla is known as *oba* or *shiso*.

In Asia, many herbs are served as *pot-herbs*, sometimes braised, as they might be in the USA, but also stir-fried or steamed. The leaves of cassava (a plant usually thought of as the source of a starchy root vegetable) are slow-cooked then puréed in the Indonesian dish *daun ubi tumbuk*. Another plant not normally thought of as a source of leafy greens is chilli – the foliage of members of the *Capsicum* genus are treated as pot-herbs in the Philippines. They don't contain capsaicin, so are not hot-tasting, like their fruits. Likewise, *lablab* (*Lablab purpureus*), or hyacinth bean – grown primarily in tropical Asia, India, Indonesia, Malaysia, Papua New Guinea and the Philippines for its protein-rich seeds – also yields leaves, sprouts and greens to be cooked as pot-herbs. *Melinjo* (*Gnetum gnemnon*) has no English name, but the shoots and leaves of this tropical tree are treated as pot-herbs in Malaysia and Java – especially in Java's traditional

Perilla (*Perilla frustescens* var. *crispa f. purpurea*), a plant that can easily reseed an entire garden.

dish *Sayur Asam* (a vegetable soup made sour with tamarind paste). Another plant, better known for its seeds, but sometimes cooked like spinach, is sesame (*Sesamum indicum*). Its leaves are braised in soy sauce as a topping for rice in Korea. The stems have a mucilaginous quality that thicken soups.

The edible chrysanthemum (*Chrysanthemum coronarium*), or *shungiku*, provides leaves and flowers for Chinese and Japanese soups, or as steamed pot-herbs, and as a chopped vegetable in Korean omelettes.

Katuk (*Sauropus androgynus*) provides flowers, leaves and tender tips that are staple foods in Borneo. The latter are especially prized and are grown for sale to high-end restaurants as far away as Hawaii (where they are now being grown) and Japan. They are served raw, or very briefly stir-fried, as 'tropical asparagus' – a misnomer that attests to their culinary potential. Katuk is indigenous to the lowland rainforests of South-east Asia. *Mitsuba* or Japanese parsley (*Cryptotaenia japonica, C. canadensis*) has three-part leaves – which suggest its synonym, 'trefoil' – and leaf stalks that are used in fried dishes, soups and stews. The leaves and leafstalks, either fresh or blanched, taste like a cross between celery and sorrel. Moringa's foliage and roots are eaten – as pot-herb and condiment, respectively – widely across Africa, South Asia and the western islands of the Pacific. Its young foliage is cooked like spinach – specifically, chopped spinach, since the leaves are so tiny – in the Philippines. Water spinach or *kangkong* (*Ipomoea aquatica*) is not related to spinach at all, but is a popular substitute from Japan and Korea all the way to Indonesia and Thailand. Usually cooked as a pot-herb, it is also eaten raw in salads.

Asians – other than the Chinese – also make use of many herbs in the form of salads. Water celery (*Oenanthe javanica* and *O. stolonifera*: Japanese: *ashitaba*; Chinese: *chin tsai, chu kuei, shui qin, sui kan*; Thai, *pak chi lawm*; Vietnamese: *rau can*), native to Asia and Australia, is used as garnish, salad green and – especially with older leaves – pot-herb. Water pepper (*Polygonum hydropiperoides*)'s young leaves are used in raw or pickled Vietnamese dishes, such as the kimchee-like *du'a can*. It tastes like rocket (arugula), with a hint of coriander. As with some of the pot-herbs mentioned above, some utilize parts of plants that Europeans don't normally consider as food. Banana flowers are eaten in salads in South-east Asia, particularly in Laos, Vietnam and Thailand.

While the rest of the world has often brewed *herbal teas* – either as medicines or as substitutes for tea or coffee – Asians have long had access to *real* tea (*Camellia sinensis*). When tea was first used, on the slopes of its native Himalayas, it was part of an energizing beverage that might have included other herbs, fat meats (such as mutton), vegetables and even salt and yak butter. That long list of other ingredients in brewed tea has since been shortened (usually to sugar, milk, lemon or honey), but some flavourings are added to the tea leaves themselves – such as petals of jasmine (*Jasminum* spp.), or chrysanthemum (*Chrysanthemum* spp.), or even some of the herbal 'teas' already mentioned.

In Russia several herbs are used to flavour *nastoika* – variously flavoured infused vodkas. One unusual nastoika gets its characteristic vanilla-like scent from buffalo grass (*Hierchloe odorata*).

Asians do use herbs in ways that are familiar to Europeans, that is, as *seasoning* ingredients. The Chinese use herbs less than most other Asians, restricting their herbal palate to coriander, spring onions and Chinese or flat-leaved chives (*Allium tuberosum*). Flat-leaved chives have a delicate garlicky aroma that lends itself to noodles, salads, soups and meat-filled dumplings.

Celery (*Apium graveolens*) is native to the temperate regions of Europe and Asia, and was probably introduced into Southeast Asia from both directions. Oddly enough, it was never adopted as a vegetable there (it is rarely allowed to grow into our familiar bundles of stalks) but is used almost exclusively as a garnish.

Elsewhere, curry leaves (*Murraya koenigii*), fresh or dried, are used as a flavouring for, of all things, curries. When fresh the leaves are pleasantly fragrant but, like many other herbs, much of their charm is lost when dried. Curry leaves are native to South-east Asia, Southern India and Sri Lanka. *Makrut*, or Kaffir lime leaf (*Citrus hystrix*), tastes – not surprisingly – like the zest of fresh limes. It is grown commercially in South-east Asia and Hawaii. 'Kaffir' is an Arabic word meaning 'foreign', 'unbeliever' or 'infidel' – a term that reflects Indonesia's association with Islam since the sixteenth century. Salam leaf, *daun salam* (*Eugenia polyantha*) is sometimes known as Indonesian bay leaf, though it is unrelated to true bay leaves. Leaves are harvested from a large tropical tree and add a flavour resembling anise, clove and lemon to dishes in Indonesia and Suriname.

As we've seen, herb use in Vietnam is extensive. A few we haven't mentioned include Vietnamese mint, *daun kesom*, *rau ram* (*Polygonum odoratum*), a fragrant herb that smells of coriander, eucalyptus and lemon, with suggestions of basil and mint. Its leaves flavour curried dishes throughout South-east Asia. Vietnamese pickled cabbage, fermented like Korean kimchee, usually contains *daun kesom*. Unfortunately, 'Vietnamese mint' is also the name of a completely unrelated plant (*rau hung cay*, a *Mentha x gracilis* hybrid) – yet another example of the confusion caused by common names. Gardeners should also beware of *rau hung cay*'s tendency to quickly overrun a garden. This Vietnamese staple tastes like peppermint, only milder, less assertive.

While many Vietnamese herbs seem to be part of the basil–mint–coriander spectrum, rice paddy herb (*Limnophilia chinensis*) adds a lemon–cumin–celery flavour to Vietnamese dishes, especially those with a sweet–sour taste. Another familiar citrus-like herb is lemongrass. It is essential in Thai and Vietnamese kitchens, where it adds the aroma of lemon zest while providing a more delicate sourness than could be obtained from actual lemon juice.

The Japanese, who have little land but a great deal of ocean, harvest large amounts of a class of plants that are under-utilized elsewhere: seaweeds. *Nori* (laver, *Porphyra* spp.) is pressed into thin sheets and dried. It's the familiar wrapping material in sushi rolls. Unlike most wrappers used in other cuisines – such as banana leaves or cornhusks – it is completely edible (the only other edible wrappers are the young grape leaves that are

Laver (*Porphyra* spp.) as prepared sheets of nori.

stuffed in Middle Eastern kitchens). Oddly enough, laver is a traditional foodstuff in only one other location: the Irish and Welsh coasts of the Irish sea – where it is baked into scone-like breads. Other seaweeds, such as *wakame* (a form of kelp, *Undaria pinnatifida*), are treated as a vegetable in Japan. The thick and leathery *kombu* (another kelp, *Laminaria japonica*) flavours *dashi*, the basic broth that is to Japanese cookery what stock is to French. *Kombu* is banned as a noxious weed in England and Scotland. *Wakame* has been commercially raised off the coast of France, for export, despite the fact that is considered a highly invasive species elsewhere, such as across the Channel in Great Britain.

The Americas

North and South America represent an amazing variety of climates and terrains, which would have supported the evolution of a vast number of indigenous species, but the fact that they have been colonized by, or received immigrants from, almost every culture in the world has made them incredibly rich in culinary traditions. It also means that the range of culinary herbs found there is astonishing. Many of the New World's plants have become staples everywhere else (beans, chillis, chocolate, maize, potatoes and tomatoes, to name a few), but here we'll consider only a few of the herbs that the hemisphere has contributed to the world's cuisines.

Herb use in the New World follows similar patterns as found elsewhere (with the exception of Vietnam, as mentioned above). Herbs serve as cooked greens (alone as a component of soups or stews), raw salads, teas and other beverages, as wrappers for other foods and as seasoning – providing tastes and aromas to dishes that might otherwise be bland.

Pot-herbs and salad herbs include lambsquarters (*Chenopodium* spp.), a relative of spinach whose leaves are cooked in much the same way. The seeds, like quinoa, are eaten as pseudo-cereals (that is, grain-like foods that are not the fruits of grasses). *C. album* is native to Europe, while *C. berlandieri* is indigenous to North America, where it was once a major part of the Native American diet, from Alaska to Mexico. Both species are found in waste places and roadsides everywhere in the temperate zone, and as unwanted guests in gardens. In Mexico, both species are used as pot-herbs, known, collectively, as *quelites*. Waterleaf (*Talinum triangulare* or *T. fruticosum*), or Surinam spinach (also *cariru*, Ceylon spinach, and a host of other names), grows in Florida, Hawaii, and the tropics everywhere. It's a major crop in Brazil. Like purslane and sorrel, it gets it a tangy, lemony flavour from oxalic acid. It is usually eaten as a salad herb.

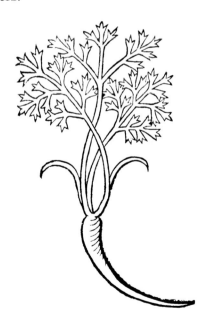

Jacob Meydenbach (printer), 'Carrot' (*Daucus carota*), from *Ortus Sanitatis*, 1491, engraving.

Teas and infusions include maté (*Ilex paraguariensis*), the most widely consumed herbal beverage in Latin America. It contains substantial amounts of caffeine, which makes it a popular stimulant. It takes its name from a drinking vessel made by Incas from a dried gourd. There are, of course, other stimulating beverages: coffee, naturally, and guarana (*Paullinia cupana*), sold in the form of soft drinks in Brazil. Both of these are brewed from berries, not herbs. Coca leaves (*Erythroxylum coca*) make energizing teas in many Andean countries, and are actually legal in only three: Bolivia, Peru and Venezuela.

Elderberry (*Sambucus nigra*) was brought to the English colonies in the New World, but another species (*S. canadensis*) was

Elderberry (*Sambucus canadensis*). The blossoms, called 'blow' in the USA, are the basis of St-Germain liqueur.

already there, and still thrives in moist waste areas, especially along rural roadsides. The leaves are toxic but the berries and flowers are not. The flowers add a delicate floral note to heavy syrup (called *Hollunder* in Germany) for use in home-made sodas, champagne cocktails and for macerating fresh strawberries. The flowers are also used in the production of the liqueur St-Germain. Elderflower wine and cordial are very popular in the UK. Elderberries used to be made into wine (they were once known as 'the English grape') and jellies, and are also an ingredient in the Italian cordial sambucca.

Linden (*Tilia* spp.) blossoms are European in origin and they are the basis of sweet herbal tisanes there and in Russia, but only in one other place: Mexico. The reason has nothing to do with the spread of the European species (*T. cordata*) however; Mexico has its own indigenous linden (*T. mexicana*). Both places discovered that the flowers made a pleasant tea independently. Mexican balm (*Agastache mexicana*), also known as *toronjil*, has an anise-like scent and makes a pleasant herbal tea. Wild rosella's flowers add flavour and colour to cool drinks and herbal teas in Jamaica, where it's called 'sorrel', and Mexico, where it's called *jamaica*. This use is almost identical to that of African cooks.

Sassafras was 'discovered' growing on an island off the coast of Massachussetts in 1602 by Bartholemew Gosnold, who brought it back to England as a tea or seasoning for soups (which mirrors its use, as *filé*, in gumbos). Sassafras also lends a delicate wintergreen flavour to root beer. Oil of wintergreen (methyl salicylate), not surprisingly, can be extracted from wintergreen (*Gaultheria* spp.) itself but also from some birches (*Betula* spp.). Root beer is a New World variation on 'dandelion and burdock' (a similar soft drink that was originally made, in England, from those named ingredients but, like root beer, is now made almost entirely from artificial ingredients). The leaves of wintergreen are brewed as tea (hence another common name, tea berry) or as a source of commercial flavourings for confectionery, chewing gum, mouthwash, tobacco and toothpaste.

Wrapping is another use of herbs in the New World. Setting aside tacos and burritos (or 'wraps', their commercial descendants), since they are part of the spectrum of starch-enclosed foods like sandwiches, dumplings and ravioli, as outside the subject of this book, tamales are the quintessential wrapped food from North and Central America. They are usually thought of as being wrapped in corn-husks (or, in canned versions, parchment paper), which is how they are made in northern Mexico, the first Mexican cuisine to travel beyond the Rio Grande. Immigration patterns have changed and now regional cuisines that were little known outside Mexico and Central America are beginning to be recognized. Banana leaves are used, instead of corn-husks, as wrappers for tamales in Oaxaca. Their size and shape allows the tamales to be larger and flatter than those made in northern Mexico. In the other direction, fresh avocado leaves (*Persea americana* subs. *drymifolia*) serve as wrappers for smaller tamales. The leaves are also used, fresh or dried, to add a faint hazelnut–liquorice flavour to bean dishes, salsas and salads.

For *seasoning, culantro* or sawleaf herb (*Eryngium foetidum*) is sometimes called Mexican coriander, because it serves as a substitute for true coriander. *Culantro* is so popular in tropical cooking that it has dozens of names from *coulante* (Haiti) to *ngò gai* (Vietnam). Like coriander, *epazote* (*Chenopodium ambrosioides*) is an acquired taste for those north of the border (many find its flavour to be reminiscent of kerosene!). Epazote, either fresh or dried, is a popular addition to beans and in some fillings for Mexican quesadillas. Not all of those who consumed the herb were interested in its culinary properties – many believed it could help them rid themselves of worms or prevent flatulence. On the latter subject:

> Virtually every culture that consumes large amounts of vegetables, especially gassy ones like beans or members of the cabbage family, has offered folk remedies for the age-old problem. They range from varying cooking techniques (such as cooking in several changes of water – which serves only to reduce the quantity of water-soluble vitamins and minerals), to additions of herbs and spices (it is interesting to note that the seasonings chosen are invariably the culture's favorites, anyway), to more arcane and mystical rituals. These solutions reveal an utterly charming optimism and trust in unverified anecdotal evidence.[8]

Mexican oregano (*Lippia graveolens*) is one of a dozen *Lippia* species called 'oregano' in Mexico. It is used much as oregano (its flavour and aroma are similar, but sharper, than those of true oregano), but it is also brewed as *té de pais* or 'country tea' in Mexico (though it grows from Nicaragua to California). The unrelated Mexican oregano (*Poliomintha longiflora*) has a bitter, aromatic quality, reminiscent of sage and wormwood, and was used in cooking by Native Americans who lived along the us–Mexican border. Another local herb, *yerba santa* (*Eriodictyon californicum*), is native to northern Mexico, California and Oregon, but now grows as far south as Brazil. It adds an aniselike, balsamic flavor to Mexican and Tex-Mex dishes. Yerba santa contains compounds called 'flavanones' that are used in the pharmaceutical industry – not because of their therapeutic properties but because they mask the bitter taste of other drugs.

Various *Allium* species (the genus that includes chives, garlic and onions) have served as seasoning almost everywhere on the planet. North America's native species is called 'ramps' (*A. tricoccum*). Ramps are found throughout the American Appalachians. One of the earliest wild edible plants, they are the focus of food festivals celebrated every spring, where they are eaten as pot-herbs, as salads and as condiments to enhance other local food favourites.

Australia, New Zealand and the South Pacific

In recent years Australian wild herbs – 'bush herbs' – have enjoyed a new level of popularity. They appear in restaurants and cookbooks with increasing frequency and some have even begun to show up in places far from the land down under. As elsewhere, Australia's herbs function as pot-herbs and salads, wrappers, herbal teas and seasonings.

The region's primary pot-herb, New Zealand spinach or warrigal greens (*Tetragonia tetragonioides* or *T. expansa*), is native to Argentina, Australia, Chile, Japan and New Zealand. Its first mention in print was in the eighteenth-century journals of Captain Cook – hence one of its other common names, Cook's cabbage. Cook found it useful in preventing scurvy. The botanist Joseph Banks brought seeds back to England in the next century. The leaves are cooked as pot-herbs, with a preliminary blanch and rinse to reduce their sour oxalates to a palatable level. It is grown all around East Asia but is considered an invasive weed in the Americas.

The only indigenous plant that provides leaves suitable for wrapping food is pandan or screw pine (*Pandanus* spp.). It is used all over the Pacific region, both as a wrapper for foods and as a flavouring agent. It has a lovely scent reminiscent of vanilla, hazelnuts and coconut, and it tints custards and rice dishes a pale jade green.

Acacias (*Acacia* spp.) are common in Australia and are often employed as herbal teas – though they have several other culinary uses as well (for example, the flowers of mudgee wattle, *A. spectabilis*, after being marinated in brandy and battered, are deep-fried to make dessert fritters). Tannins in the leaves add a pleasant astringency and the flowers have a lovely violet-like scent. Their tannins provide bittering to some beers in place of hops. Acacia seeds (especially those of wattle-seed, *A. decurrens*, *A. floribunda*, and *A. longifolia*) are often roasted to liberate flavours of chocolate, coffee and hazelnut.

Lemon myrtle (*Backhousia citriodora*) is another of the Australian 'bush herbs' that can be brewed as herbal tea. It is used like lemongrass or lemon verbena despite the fact that its scent is closer to lime than lemon.

Many bush herbs lend themselves well to use as garnishes or seasonings. Aniseed myrtle (*Backhousia anisata*) tastes like liquorice – even though it's not related to any of the other plants that exhibit that flavour (anise; fennel; liquorice, *Glycyrrhiza glabra*; or star anise, *Illicium verum*). The leaves garnish desserts, especially those containing cream or fruits, such as apricots or pears.

Blue gum (*Eucalyptus globulus*), a Tasmanian tree, has a smell similar to cajuput (*Melaleuca leucadendra*), which led Baron Ferdinand von Müller to recommend its use as a preventative of fever.[9] It was taken to Algeria in the nineteenth century to deal with fevers there, and it worked – though not for the reasons he imagined. The trees' root systems were so effective at extracting moisture that they effectively drained the marshes where the fever-carrying mosquitoes bred. There are at least fourteen eucalyptus species in Australia that have 'peppermint' in their common names, despite the fact that none of them contain menthol. Their flavour is more tonic and astringent.

Lemon aspen (*Acronychia acidula*)'s leaves offer a grape-fruit–lime flavour, with less acidity than either fruit. Native to Australia, it is found throughout the Pacific Islands and Indonesia.

Mints are not always mint in Australia – the name is com-monly attached to any number of non-*Mentha* species. River mint (*M. australis*), also known as native mint, is one of seven true mints that *are* indigenous to Australia. This spearmint-like plant grows wild and – like all mints – can easily take over any garden in which it's planted. Native mints (*Prostanthera* spp.) – not including the one mentioned above, are but more examples of the duplication of common names – 'native mint' also refers, in Australia, to many peppermint-scented species of eucalyp-tus. *Prostanthera* is part of the same family as mint, *Lamiaceae*, and shares some characteristics with *Mentha*. All of these plants provide a minty flavour to foods prepared by Aborigines (and others). Some native mints are: round-leaf mintbush (*P. rotundifolia*), snowy mintbush (*P. nivea*) and Victorian christmas bush (*P. lasianthos*).

Native pepper (*Drimys lanceolata*) serves – not surprisingly – as pepper, but, in addition to the deep purple berries, the leaves are also used. Native pepper is hotter than *Piper nigrum*, but its heat comes on gradually. The berries colour white sauces a pale mauve, but leaves can be used if that colour is undesired. Native pepper is added near the end of cooking, as its flavour dissipates with prolonged exposure to heat. Related species include dorrigo pepper (*Tasmannia stipitata*) and pepper tree (*T. insipida*).

Obviously, humans have valued certain flavourful weeds from time immemorial. Not content to find them in the wild, they've carefully transplanted them to herb gardens and purposely carried them to the far corners of the globe. Weeds themselves, not content to stay on the rocky hillsides where they first grew, have benefited from the peripatetic nature of *Homo sapiens* – sometimes as welcome fellow travellers, sometimes as stowaways.

4

The Sisterhood of the Travelling Plants

Herbs have spread around the world as part of human trade and migrations. Some moved around the Old World with human assistance – many long before our history began to be recorded. In some cases we only know this occurred because we can trace the history recorded in their DNA. For example, the *lablab* that lends its name to a dish in Indonesia has long been considered indigenous to that area, but recent studies have shown that its wild ancestors came from tropical Africa, where they still thrive. Apparently some ancient traveller had the foresight to carry some of the seeds along with his or her other provisions. Oddly enough, this Asian staple is virtually unknown as a foodstuff in sub-Saharan Africa, where it originated.

Richard Hakluyt's *Divers Voyages Touching the Discovery of America and the Islands Adjacent* (1582) advised travellers to take along a copy of Wylliam Turner's *A New Herball* (1551).[1] A provisions list, a little later (1630), included a few necessary spices – cinnamon, cloves, mace, nutmeg and pepper – but didn't mention herbs.[2] Presumably such travellers would automatically also bring seeds for essential herbs for planting in their new locations.

When the pilgrims began scouting, in 1620, for a place to set up their new settlement, they first made a listing of useful wild plants that were already growing there. Among them, they noted sorrel, watercress and yarrow. John Winthrop, a physician at Plymouth, ordered herb seeds for use there in 1631. He spent £160 sterling – a vast sum in those days – on some 48 species, including alexanders (*Smyrnium olustratum*), angelica, borage, chervil, clary sage, hyssop, parsley, rosemary, sage and thyme. His order also included bugloss (*Echium vulgare*), dock, ox-eye daisies (*Leucanthemum vulgare*) and lamb's lettuce (*Valerianella locusta*) – which soon escaped to become common weeds and 'wildflowers' in the New World.

Salem, Massachusetts, was an early scion of the nearby pilgrim colony at Plymouth. In 1629 the new community requested a number of seeds, rootstocks and vines from their masters, the Massachusetts Bay Company. Some were practical herbs used for dyeing fabric, such as woad (*Isatis tinctoria*) and madder (*Rubia tinctorum*), but the request for hop-roots was clearly culinary – in England hops had replaced other bittering herbs used in making beer in around 1600.

Dutch settlers in New York's Hudson Valley – like their English neighbours – brought along their familiar kitchen herbs: chives, marjoram, parsley, rosemary, summer savory, tarragon and thyme. Parsley seems to have been the herb most

Otto Brunfels, 'Wild ginger' (*Asarum europaeum*), *Herbarium Vivae Eicones*, 1530, engraving.

Ibn Butlan, 'Leeks' (*Allium porrum*), from *Tacuinum Sanitatis*,
c. 1380–1400.

used by the Dutch colonists, not just in New Netherland, but in Africa, the Caribbean and the East Indies. Spices were much more frequently noted in their recipes – though *De Verstandige Kock* ('The Sensible Cook'), a cookbook originally published in 1667 and later included in *Het Vermakelijct Landleven* (1683), includes recipes that incorporated celery leaves and sorrel. These were books that would have been well known among the wealthier Dutch colonists, providing a taste of home – and the good life – in distant colonies. One dish in *De Verstandige Kock*, unusual by modern standards, called for the large leaves of borage (or clary sage or bugloss) to be dipped in egg, then fried and finally dusted with sugar. It was served as a side dish for ham or other pork.[3]

Further south, John Bartram – a Pennsylvania Quaker – was appointed Botanizer Royal for America, in 1765, by King George III.[4] Bartram was responsible for sending some 200

Bergamot (*Monarda didyma*), visited by a Silver-spotted Skipper (*Epargyreus clarus*).

native plants from America to England. He discovered, and was first to raise, two species of wild herbs: black cohosh (*Cimicifuga racemosa*) and Oswego tea, a bergamot (*Monarda didyma*). Linnaeus described this simple, uneducated farmer as 'the greatest natural botanist in the world'.[5] Bartram's researches took him far from his home, which was then just outside Philadelphia: south to Florida, north to Lake Ontario and west to the Ohio River.[6]

Bartram established the first botanical garden in the New World. Today's botanical gardens appear very different from Bartram's – their look is based on architectural and aesthetic notions that didn't exist for another century (such as those of landscape designers Frederick Law Olmsted and Calvert Vaux). His garden was created to aid in his research. Among the herbs he planted there were agrimony (*Agrimonia eupatoria*), basil, bay leaf, borage, catnip, chamomile, chives, comfrey (*Symphytum officinale*), dill, fennel, germander (*Teucrium chamaedrys*), horehound, hyssop, lavender, lovage, myrtle

William Turner, 'Mugwort' (*Artemisia vulgaris*), from *A New Herball* (1551), engraving.

(*Myrtus communis*), mints, sage, sweet flag, sweet woodruff, tansy, tarragon, thyme and yarrow.

Asa Gray, the founder of American systematic botany, visited the herbarium of Linnaeus in London in the 1830s. While there he saw American plant specimens that Bartram had collected nearly a century earlier. Bartram's garden still exists, on the Bartram homestead, within modern Philadelphia's city limits.

Weeds Will Be Weeds

Once, in a letter to fellow horticulturalist Philip Miller (1691–1771), Bartram complained about a number of weeds that plagued gardeners then, as now.[7] His rogue's list included chickweed, dandelion, dock, purslane, saponaria (*Saponaria officinalis*) and sorrel (*Oxalis* spp.) – all plants that had found their way from the Old World to the New. While the herbs were often brought along purposely, sometimes they travelled along on their own – they are weeds, after all.

Aside from their tendency to spread on their own, what is it that sets 'weeds' apart from other plants? Sometimes it's their sheer fecundity. Weeds will grow anywhere, outpacing and competing with plants we *want* to thrive – such as our crops and flowers. How do they manage to outgrow our native plants? According to the US Department of Agriculture (USDA), 'introduced plants are likely to invade or become noxious since they lack co-evolved competitors and natural enemies to control their populations'.[8]

From an evolutionary standpoint weeds are great success stories. The farmer's or horticulturalist's point of view is somewhat less enthusiastic. The vigorous growth of these introduced species makes them especially good at claiming

P. A. Mattioli, trans., *Les commentaries sur les six livres de la matiere medecinale de Pedacius Dioscuride*, 1565, engraving.

disturbed soils as their own. The tilled soil of domestic agriculture, unfortunately, is prime 'disturbed soil' for weeds. Roadsides and abandoned lots are other examples of disturbed soil and most of the plants that colonize such places are weeds, many of which are either known Old World herbs or plants that possess some of the desirable characteristics of culinary herbs. The wild fennel that grows everywhere in San Francisco is a perfect example.

Sometimes the migration of herbs had an entirely different destination: oblivion. As mentioned in chapter Two, the ancient Greeks and Romans were especially fond of the herb they called *silphium*. It was native to the Greek province of Cyrenaica, in what is now northeastern Libya, but had been driven to extinction by the first century CE. Today we don't even know what the plant was, but it must have had a garlicky taste, since the Romans used asafoetida, *Ferula foetida*, as a substitute.

From the Old to the New

Many herbs brought from the Old World naturalized themselves to become common weeds in the New. Our roadsides and waste places would have looked very different before the explorers, conquistadors, pilgrims and other colonists arrived.

Among the ones that were transported on purpose are several herbs that served as medicines. *Achillea*, at least some species, is native in much of North America, Europe and Eurasia, and includes iva (*A. moschata*) and yarrow – but they were brought to the New World anyway, for use in treating wounds, and have been introduced in Hawaii. Catnip, like many medicinal herbs brought to the New World, soon escaped to do some colonizing of its own, eventually covering most of North America. Common plantain (*Plantago major*) is native to Europe and North Africa – the Ancient Egyptians called it *asoeth*. Young leaves are occasionally eaten as pot-herbs, but it was brought to the USA for its alleged medical properties. It was said to be good for everything from the bites of mad dogs and rattlesnakes, through asthma to eye problems. Native Americans called it 'white man's foot' because they found that it grew everywhere the newcomers walked – which makes it a curse for those who prefer their lawns to consist only of grass.

The subspecies of dandelion (*T. officinale* officinale) is a European native, and is the one most commonly found all over North America. Another subspecies (*T. officinale* ceratophorum) is native to the North American continent, but it is only found in the western states and Canadian provinces.

Dandelions were known for their supposed medicinal qualities at least as far back as Avicenna, which is why colonists brought them to the New World. However, its parachute-like seeds allowed it to become one of our most common weeds and, like plantain, an annoyance to lawn-lovers everywhere. Purslane (*Portulaca oleracea*) is native to India, but is a weed virtually everywhere. It is a popular salad or pot-herb in Europe, and nearly made it as a trendy herb in the USA in the 1980s because of its healthy supply of vitamin E and omega-3 fatty acids. However, it never really caught on. Perhaps its former use as a survival food (it was once known as 'miner's lettuce') prevented it from earning its proper respect and glamour.

Horehound was native to England and the Mediterranean region. Brought by early colonists as a medicinal herb, the plant has now naturalized itself throughout the temperate parts of Asia, Europe, North Africa and North America. Rue is native to lands around the Mediterranean and the Canary Islands. While the Romans loved it as a culinary herb, it was spread more often as a medicinal plant.

Eucalypti of various species are Australian plants that have become naturalized in warmer parts of the USA. Blue gum is considered invasive in California. Swamp mahogany (*E. robusta* Sm.) is found in Florida. Both species are considered to be potentially dangerous alien plants in Hawaii.

Some plants served as both medical and culinary herbs, so were among the first plants carried by colonists to new regions. Saponaria, also known as soapwort or bouncing bet, is found in every US state except for Alaska and Hawaii (Colorado lists it as a noxious weed). It is indigenous in Europe and the Near East, where the only culinary use we've found is as an emulsifier in the production of halvah. Sage is certainly a well-known culinary herb, though its species name, *officinalis* (and the feminine equivalent, *officinale*) reveals its inclusion in the ancient lists of medicinal plants. It was its supposed use in medicine that led to it being spread to all parts of the temperate world. Verticillate mallow (*Malva verticillata*) is another common salad and pot-herb in southern Europe that was brought to the USA for medicinal purposes but has escaped and is now a weed from Canada south to Pennsylvania and as far west as South Dakota.

Other herbs were brought specifically for their use in the kitchen. Bergamot travelled to the New World with European colonists but the trip wasn't necessary. There was already a lovely species here: the thyme-scented lavender wild bergamot (*Monarda fistulosa*) can be seen along highways all over the eastern USA every summer. Borage originated near the eastern Mediterranean but was spread throughout Europe in classical times. It was mentioned by Dioscorides and Pliny and had certainly reached Great Britain by 1265. John Winthrop listed it among the plants he brought to New England for use in establishing the Massachusetts Bay Colony in 1630.[9] Chamomile came originally from the Azores, Northern Africa and western Europe, but is now found in temperate areas everywhere. Chamomile and several closely related plants are used primarily in herbal teas. It is known as *manzanilla de Castilla* in Colombia, which suggests that Colombians, at least, think of it as a Spanish herb. Chamomile has been carried to Australia, South Asia and North America, where it has escaped cultivation and become naturalized.

Chicory is another Mediterranean herb. It was familiar to the Romans (Horace mentioned in one of his odes). Its lovely blue flowers brighten the edges of highways in the USA, North Africa and Australia, where they have become thoroughly naturalized.

Coriander was well known to the ancient inhabitants of the eastern end of the Mediterranean – it's mentioned on

Tricoloured sage (*Salvia officinalis* 'Tricolor'), in the Brooklyn Botanical Gardens, New York.

early clay tablets from Mesopotamia. Its use spread to Europe primarily through contact with Islam, through trade and by migration of Moors into Spain. The Spaniards, in turn, brought it to the New World. Cuban oregano (*Plectranthus amboinicus*) is neither Cuban nor oregano – it's closely related to coleus, and originally grew in the East Indies; it still grows wild in Malaysia. It has become an important herb in the West Indies, however, and is cultivated all over South Asia. It has a strong thyme scent that lends itself to sauces for grilled fish and goat and Cuban black bean soup.

Dill is native to temperate Europe but has been brought to every continent except Antarctica (though it is probably there, dried, in spice jars). It is used in cuisines as different as those of India, Scandinavia and Vietnam. In Vietnam it is

W. Beach,
'Chamomile'
(*Matricaria* spp.),
from *The American
Practice Condensed, or
the Family Physician;
Being the Scientific
System of Medicine;
on Vegetable
Principles, Designed
for all Classes*
(1849), engraving.

Cuban oregano (*Plectranthus amboinicus*) is popular all over the Caribbean, where it's also known as country borage, Greek oregano, false oregano, French Tobago thyme, Spanish thyme and Stygian thyme.

known as *thi la*, and is always used cooked (unlike most other Vietnamese herbs). Fennel is native to Mediterranean Europe but has spread throughout the temperate world. It thrives in weedy lots in California's San Francisco, which may be one of the reasons for the city's signature dish (no, not Rice-a-Roni): *cioppino*, a local take on Marseille's bouillabaisse. Garlic mustard (*Alliaria petiolata*), a European weed, has invaded two-thirds of the USA and half of Canada, overwhelming native and garden plants alike. Its only redeeming grace is that it makes a good, if bitter, early season pot-herb.

Kinh gioi is native to the lower reaches of the Himalayas, but is now found from China to Europe. It has been recognized as a weed in the USA since 1889. The astringent lemony taste of the leaves and seeds make it popular in Vietnamese cooking. Lemongrass is native to Southern India and Sri Lanka but is now grown in frost-free areas around the world, and in greenhouses elsewhere. A key ingredient in the foods of Thailand and Vietnam, it is also used in Nigerian and Greek teas and soups, as a herbal tea in Mexico (*té limon* does not contain lemons – it is flavoured only with lemongrass) and as a commercial flavouring everywhere. It's impossible to imagine Thai cookery without it. Easily grown, it can escape to become a garden pest in hospitable climates, so it is best grown in containers.

William Turner, 'Dill' (*Anethum graveolens*), from *A New Herball* (1551), engraving.

Rembert Dodoens, from *A Niewe Herballe* (1578), trans. Henry Lyte.

Otto Brunfels,
'Comfrey'
(*Symphytum
officinale*), from
*Herbarium Vivae
Eicones* (1530),
engraving.

Marijuana, originally from Central Asia, has been naturalized – to the dismay of law-enforcement officials – almost
everywhere. In the USA five states (Illinois, Minnesota, Missouri,
Pennsylvania and West Virginia) have prohibited it as a noxious
weed but all states ban its intentional planting. The earliest
written reference to it is Chinese; it was listed in Shen Nung's
Pharmacopoeia in 2730 BCE.[10]

Mints, native to the Mediterranean region, have been
carried all over the world, and become a nuisance to unwitting
gardeners who thought they might make a pleasant addition
to their gardens. They soon discover that its stolons spread the
plant so rapidly that it is almost impossible to eradicate. Mints

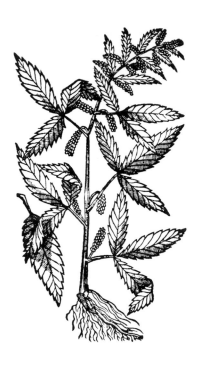

J. Pillehotte Lyon,
'Marijuana'
(*Cannabis sativa*),
from *Histoire des
Drogues* (1619),
engraving.

are found as weeds in moist areas near human habitations, or places that, long ago, were inhabited by imprudent gardeners.

Mitsuba, or Japanese parsley, is native to Asia but it has become naturalized in Hawaii. Mustards are indigenous to Asia but were spread across Europe in ancient times, and later to the New World and islands of the Pacific. Mustard serves as herb and a spice virtually everywhere since it thrives in almost any disturbed soil, easily becoming weedy, and requires practically no attention from gardeners – except trying to keep it from taking over. Before spice trade routes to Asia were established and the discovery of the Americas, mustards (and related horseradish) provided Europe's only 'hot' spices.

Perilla, introduced from China and South-east Asia, is now a pernicious weed in the eastern USA and Ontario. This annual is often planted for its ruffled crimson foliage but its prolific self-seeding soon takes over any garden. Purslane, native to Iran, has been cultivated in Southern Europe and is now a cosmopolitan weed throughout North Africa, the Americas, Asia and Australia. In Arizona it is listed as a prohibited noxious weed.

Queen Anne's lace is a familiar roadside weed that has been introduced to the USA from Europe. This progenitor of all domestic carrots is found in most American states and sub-Arctic Canadian provinces (it's considered a noxious weed in Iowa, Michigan, Ohio and Washington). Rosemary, according to some accounts, was introduced to England in

Variegated mint (*Mentha x gracilis* 'Variegata') at Clermont Historic Garden, Germantown, New York.

the fourteenth century as a gift to Queen Philippa, wife of Edward III, but it was probably already there, since Romans had occupied the island long before.[11]

Sorrel is native to the temperate regions of Europe and Asia but it has escaped from gardens to grow wild – where it is a welcome early spring green. Stinging nettles, another early spring green, came from Northern Europe, but have been naturalized as weeds in waste places throughout the north-eastern two-thirds of the US and many other temperate areas of the world. Adult plants are obnoxious but young ones provide tasty spring pot-herbs. Tansy, useful as an old-fashioned bittering agent for home-brewed beers, is native to Asia and Europe, but has been introduced and naturalized throughout North America.

Water spinach has been introduced into the USA from its native East Asia. Unfortunately, it has succeeded all too well

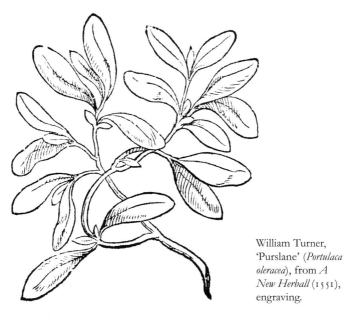

William Turner, 'Purslane' (*Portulaca oleracea*), from *A New Herball* (1551), engraving.

Queen Anne's Lace (*Daucus carota*). The seeds of this common roadside weed have a warm taste, similar to the seeds of caraway.

– and is now listed as a 'noxious weed' in Florida and Texas. Watercress, originally a European plant, has been introduced to temperate regions around the world. It's another aquatic weed found in every US state except Alaska, Hawaii and North Dakota, and in all of Canada south of Alaska. In Connecticut it is banned as an invasive species.

Wormwood and mugwort are both native to Europe and Northern Asia but have been introduced into the USA. Southernwood is indigenous to the Mediterranean region but was introduced to North America by 1672.[12] Wormwood is considered a weed in most of the states north of

Tansy (*Tanacetum vulgarum* 'Crispum'), thriving in a garden in Stamford, Connecticut.

Oklahoma, and a noxious weed in Colorado, North Dakota and Washington. Mugwort is now found in most of eastern and far western North America and is listed as 'an invasive exotic pest' in Tennessee.

The last category of travelling herbs includes one that hitched a ride on its own. Beggar ticks (*Bidens pilosa*), or Spanish needle, may be a foodstuff in many parts of the world, but is an introduced weed in much of the USA and Canada. It is reviled for exactly the same reason it got there – its seeds cling to anything that brushes against the plant and have to be forcibly removed.

Other Directions

Naturally, not all herbs travelled westward from the eastern hemisphere; many went along on the return trip and others

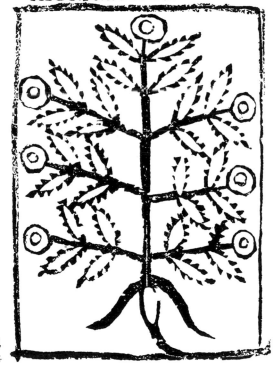

HERBA ARTEMISIA LFPTA,
FILOS.I.MATRICALE.

Apuleius Platonicus, 'Mugwort' (*Artemisia vulgaris*), *Herbarium Apuleii Platonici*, 1481, engraving.

travelled from one part of the Old World to another – some by invitation, and still others came as welcome guests, only to become unwanted weeds.

Most of the weeds used as herbs in Great Britain and Europe have been there for so many centuries that they're treated as if they were indigenous. There are a number of invasive plants that have been imported, intentionally or otherwise, from the New World, Asia and Australia, but most of them have no culinary uses. The only exceptions are some edible seaweeds (mentioned elsewhere).

Plants that were carried intentionally to the Old World include angelica, which came originally from Scandinavia and northeastern Asia, but had been naturalized in the rest of Europe by the sixteenth century. Bananas (*Musa* spp.) are native to Africa but seventeenth-century Spanish and Portuguese traders brought them to Asia and tropical parts of the Americas. The flowers are eaten in India, Sri Lanka and the countries of South-east Asia. The leaves are used as plates in India and as wrappers for steamed or baked foods in several places. The local tamales in Oaxaca, Mexico are wrapped in banana leaves; they are also filled with *mole poblano* – a rich braised mixture of chillis, chocolate, raisins, nuts and turkey (or chicken) – or *rajas* (strips of roasted poblano chiles) and cheese.

Basil was originally a wild plant in tropical Asia but it was already familiar to the Ancient Greeks, who called it *ókimon*. It is now grown around the world. Plus, in Africa, there's partminger (*Ocimum canum*) and, in South America, Peruvian basil (*O. micranthum*). Moringa (*Moringa* ssp.) – at least its early ancestors – originated in Africa and some thirteen species are still eaten there. Ancient Egyptians used one species (*M. pterygosperma*) medicinally. However, the genus diversified both naturally and through domestication in India, becoming *M. oleifera* in the Himalayan foothills.[13]

Cassava (*Manihot esculenta*) is indigenous to Brazil's rain-forests, but had already spread as a cultivated crop all over South and Central America and the Caribbean by the time the Portuguese and Spanish arrived in the early sixteenth century. The Portuguese brought it to West Africa and on to South and South-east Asia, and Spanish ships carried it to the Philippines. Europeans were primarily interested in the starchy roots, which give us our tapioca, as a source of calories for colonial labourers, but the natives themselves also made use of the leaves. Oddly enough, the Indonesian name for this pot-herb is *daun Perancis*, which translates to 'French leaf'. The term is not historically or botanically accurate but it does acknowledge that cassava is foreign, even after it has been growing in Indonesia for 500 years.

Edible chrysanthemums are, like most chrysanthemums, native to Europe and western Asia but are only considered to be a foodstuff in eastern Asia (China, Japan, Korea and the Philippines). Lemon verbena is native to South America (Argentina, Bolivia, Brazil, Chile, Paraguay, Peru and Uruguay). The Spanish carried it home in the early seventeenth century, calling it *hierba luisa*. It has since been spread to frost-free areas (and greenhouses) around the world. Another edible flower species, marigolds (*Tagetes* spp.), are New World plants from temperate regions of South America. Once carried back to Europe by seventeenth-century Spaniards, they now have worldwide distribution. In frost-free regions they naturalize. The flowers add colour and a slight liquorice flavor to herbal teas, rice dishes and some soups and stews, but all parts of the plant can be used. Tagetes oil is a commercial flavouring. Yet another culinary flower is roselle, which is native to southern Asia, from India east to Malaysia. The red calyxes have been prized in Africa longer than historical records have been kept and Africa still exports most of the world's supply. Roselle arrived in the western hemisphere, possibly as a result of the slave trade, before the seventeenth century. Its use has since spread throughout South and Central America, north to Mexico and the Caribbean and west to Hawaii and the Philippines. It has been grown sporadically in Florida but since even the slightest frost kills it it must be treated as an annual.

Papayas (*Carica papaya*) are native to tropical Central America but are now grown in similar climates around the world. Generally, the fruits are the desired part of the plant, but in Indonesia the greens and flowers are steamed as pot-herbs (the flowers are less bitter than the leaves). The normally discarded seeds have a delightful peppery quality that suggest that they would be good in a salad or as a garnish.

Tea, which is indigenous to the cool lower slopes of the Himalayan mountains, travelled in ancient times to China and on to Japan. In most of the places to which tea was exported only the dried leaves were taken; seeds went only to Japan and the South Asian regions that could grow the little bushes. Europeans first heard of tea from sixteenth-century travel accounts (oddly enough, Marco Polo never mentioned Chinese tea drinking), notably those of Jan Hugo van Linschooten, a Dutch citizen who first visited India, on a Portuguese ship, in 1595. Shortly thereafter the Portuguese were banned from the Indian ports and seven years later the Dutch East India Company was formed to control the area and its trade. Five years later the company brought tea to Java, and to Holland for the first time in 1610. Most tea continued to be shipped from China and, some time later, it began to be drunk in England. Samuel Pepys, in his diary entry for 25 September 1660, wrote, 'I did send for a cup of tea (a China drink), of which I never had drank before.' It was the first beverage he mentioned that was *not* alcoholic (before tea and coffee, beer was the safest way to drink water, because boiling was part of the beer-making process). Thomas Twining opened a tea shop in London in 1706 but tea did not become really popular in England until after 1713, when the newly formed East India Company began bringing regular shipments from Canton. By 1750 the company was importing 18,500 tons per year.

Plants that were carried intentionally from the New World but became naturalized – sometimes becoming invasive and unwanted pests – include *cang cua (Peperomia pellucida)*, native to northern South America, naturalized in Alabama, Florida, Georgia, Hawaii, Louisiana and Texas – and South-east Asia (it's popular in Vietnam). Culantro (*Eryngium foetidum*) was originally a plant of tropical Central America. It's now a weed known as spiritweed in Florida, Georgia, Hawaii, Puerto Rico and the Virgin Islands. It also thrives in Africa, South America and South-east Asia. Around the Caribbean it has names like *culantro de burro, culantro de cimarron, culantro de coyote, culantro de montana* and *culantro del monte* – names which are sometimes applied to another species (*Peperomia acuminata*). The various 'culantros' and 'cilantro' (coriander) sound similar because they are used in similar ways. Each of these three species can be found around the Caribbean and Gulf of Mexico. Several different cultures occupy that relatively small area but they have all been touched by Spanish conquest and colonialism. The Spanish had learned to use coriander from the Moors and brought their taste for the herb to the New World, even though the original plant did not always thrive in the tropical climate. No doubt they applied the name of their familiar plant to other species that could be substituted as they moved from place to place.

Epazote originated in tropical regions of the Americas but has now spread to temperate regions everywhere; it is found in Ontario, Nova Scotia and Quebec in eastern Canada, as well as every US state except Alaska, Minnesota, Montana,

'Marjoram' (*Origanum majorana*), from the Arabic version of Dioscorides' *De Materia Medica*.

North Dakota and Wyoming. In most of these places it is considered invasive. By the eighteenth century it was being brewed as tea in Germany, where it was known as *jesuitentee*, *karthäusertee* and, expressing the obvious, *mexicanisches teekraut*. Marjoram first grew in northern Africa and western Asia but was already a familiar herb for the ancient Greeks and Romans. It was introduced into the New World but – other than a single unsubstantiated reference to it being a common weed in New York's Catskills – it seems to exist as a naturalized species only in Massachusetts and Pennsylvania.

As these peripatetic plants found new homes in distant countries – with or without our intentional assistance – they altered the cooking habits of the people who lived there, and their recipes.

5
The Herbal Melting Pot

When cultures first encounter each other they invariably exchange ingredients and cooking techniques. People have been moving around and taking their notions about food with them for as long as they have been people. While the encounter may be colonial in nature (hence economically and politically advantageous to only one of the cultures) each is made richer – at least in the culinary sense. Who could imagine the food of Italy without the New World's tomatoes, or Thai dishes without Europe's basil, or Indian food without hot peppers from South America? While some xenophobes strive to preserve 'authentic' regional dishes, their efforts are, ultimately, futile. *All* food is fusion food.

Often immigrants bring along their own food traditions and ingredients (or at least seeds). Generally, these newcomers are not welcomed warmly into their new communities and their foods are dismissed as weird, unpalatable, not fit for human consumption (by which they mean not fit for their *own* consumption). The immigrant's foods are used as markers that define the newly arrived social or ethnic group as somehow less than human. Ironically, the infusion of new ingredients and techniques from abroad almost always makes the food of the new country more interesting.

The same can often be said of wars. In fact, the broadening of the culinary arts may be the *only* lasting benefit that military actions provide to both victors and vanquished. Soldiers (and sailors) are invariably placed in unfamiliar places and contexts and they don't get *all* of their sustenance from their rations. They are exposed to people who eat very different foods from their own. When they return to their homelands they bring newly acquired tastes with them. Participants in, and resisters of, the Vietnam War (as well as their Second World War-era parents) provide good examples of the positive effect of conflict upon cuisine.

At home, in the 1960s, non-combatant baby boomers were involved in an exploration of (among other things) many different ethnic cuisines. Interest in Indian religion and philosophy led to an interest in Indian cooking. Anti-war identification with the peoples of South-east Asia led to an exploration of *their* cuisines (in an odd parallel to that being done by the servicemen in the same area).

After the Vietnam War ended many Vietnamese moved to the USA. Like many ethnic groups before them, they opened restaurants selling the foods they knew from 'the old country' in the new one. As is always the case when cuisines relocate in new areas, cooks must make adjustments: ingredients and/or cooking techniques have to be modified to suit new conditions. So, while Vietnamese tables always included large amounts of fresh herbs to be added, as condiments, by each diner, sorrel (*Rumex scutatus*) – an unfamiliar European herb – became part of the mix. There was no word for it in Vietnamese, so they just called it *rau chua* (meaning 'sour herb') or *rau thom* ('fresh herb').

Vietnamese coffee (iced, as *ca phe sua da*, or warm as *ca phe sura nong*) is another example of a 'fusion' recipe that is considered to be an 'authentic' regional speciality. Coffee originally grew in Ethiopia. Since Islamic law forbids consumption of alcohol, coffee became the social beverage of choice among Muslims in the fifteenth century (the word 'coffee' is derived from the Arabic word for wine: *qahwah*). Within a century its use spread to all of Europe and on to European colonies in the New World. As it could not be grown in temperate climates the plants were smuggled to many other tropical locations (our slang term 'java' is a reflection of coffee's expanded range). As an expensive import, Europeans (especially the French, who had a limited colonial presence in the coffee-growing locations of the time) looked around for ways to maximize the small amount of coffee they could afford. They did it by adulterating it with the dried and roasted roots of a common wild herb that grew at home: chicory. That French preference is still felt in former French colonies, such as Louisiana and, later, in what came to be known as French Indochina. Today, the Vietnamese (especially expatriates, who adapt to whatever is available in their new countries) may be the second largest producers of coffee in the world, but many still prefer their coffee combined with chicory – neither plant indigenous in their country.

The war in South-east Asia also led to changes in Australian food. Today, in Melbourne, one can find such atypical 'Australian' dishes as banana blossom salad with shredded pork. This is because Laotian refugees from the conflicts brought a taste for that dish with them when they left for a new, safer, homeland. One might also ask how Laotians even knew about an African plant like bananas. Banana flowers are a 'traditional Laotian ingredient' because Portuguese ships brought them from Africa's western coast in the early seventeenth century.

The post-Second World War period engendered a larger migration of people and jobs, in all directions, than in any other period in history – the Allies learned that their neighbours and co-workers could be from *anywhere*. This meant that people from, for example, New England, got to taste barbecue and the precursors of Tex-Mex cuisine for the first time. The English, French and Italians were exposed to American dishes. American soldiers brought home their newly acquired taste for pizza (with the result that dried oregano became an American staple).

In addition the post-Second World War period saw an immense surge in world travel. When the war ended factories that had been producing tanks and bombers switched to cars and commercial aeroplanes. To encourage people to buy and use their new cars, better highways was built in America and Europe, and people began visiting places they had only heard of before – and, while they were on the road, they ate. They tried hitherto unknown foods and started to think that these regional foods were somehow part of a larger cuisine. In Italy a notion evolved that was totally unfamiliar: *Italian food* (most Italians still think of dishes from the next village as *foreign food*).

Relatively low-cost flights took people to places where they were exposed to ingredients and flavours they had never known before. The middle-class parents of the hippies and soldiers were discovering 'world cuisine' on their vacations and at home on the new TV cooking shows. Restaurants became entertainment and, in order to grab the 'audience's' attention, had to look for more and more exotic foodstuffs. Herbs and spices offered excitement at a relatively low cost.

None of this was really new, of course. Human history has been one long series of exchanges and incorporation of formerly foreign foodstuffs by people who could never have predicted such culinary miscegenation. Eventually, after resisting the expected corruption of cultural purity, even the most hidebound traditionalists find themselves adopting part of the foreigners' food ways, making them their own. They don't even realize that dishes they consider to be 'ethnic' have actually been invented in their own country. In the USA dishes like chilli con carne, spaghetti and meatballs and corned beef and cabbage are not foreign at all. They are 'as American as apple pie', despite the fact that apple pie itself is not an American invention. British 'curries' are, likewise, not Indian at all – they are purely English, even if they make use of spices that never grew in the UK.

Pho, the national dish of Vietnam, is a classic fusion food. The Vietnamese didn't really eat beef (as in India, cattle were too valuable as work animals to be eaten) until the French occupied their country in the mid-nineteenth century. The rice noodles and ginger reflect Chinese influences on Vietnamese cooking that are older. Fresh chillies, obviously, are New World contributions – probably first brought by the Portuguese in the early seventeenth century. The fresh herbs, however, tossed in at the last moment at the whim of the eager soon-to-be slurper, are purely Vietnamese.

Fusion cooking is neither new nor unusual, it is the essential means by which cuisines grow and change, and it has always been so. During the 1960s and early '70s exposure to a host of formerly unfamiliar world cuisines led to some remarkable changes in the Euro-American diet. Coriander provides a perfect example of this sort of culinary change.

The Coriander Complex

The seeds of this plant, originally native to the Mediterranean region, have been a staple in European kitchens for thousands of years, and naturally travelled with Europeans to all their far-flung colonies. They were used in baked goods and in pickles and not much else. In the mid-1960s some recipes, especially those in Chinese cookbooks for Western cooks, began mentioning something called 'Chinese parsley', usually accompanied by a note advising home cooks to 'substitute parsley' – a sign that consumers had trouble finding this rare ingredient in ordinary supermarkets.

Anyone who had actually *tasted* 'Chinese parsley' would have known that regular parsley was a completely inadequate substitution. However, most Euro-American cooks would not have known the difference back then. Within a decade, all that had changed. 'Chinese parsley' had become 'coriander' ('cilantro') and had become an accepted item in Western kitchens – though there were still some 'gourmets' who complained that the herb tasted 'soapy'. There may *still* be people who feel that way, but the herb is so widely accepted that few people voice that opinion any more.

What caused the change? A widespread exposure to new cuisines, for one thing. Changes in regulations and ease of travel led to a sudden increase in the number of Chinese emigrating to Western countries, with the result that Chinese restaurants began serving something much more akin to the food in China than the typical 'Chinese' fare that had been common since the 1920s. Suddenly, non-Chinese diners knew that there was something beyond the so-called 'Cantonese' dishes to which they had become accustomed. They began seeking spots that served 'Mandarin' and 'Szechuan' dishes. Today, we would call them 'Beijing' or 'Sichuan', but we also know about the styles of Fukien, Hunan and other regional Chinese cooking styles.

Along with changes in Chinese immigration, wars in South-east Asia and Africa led to more arrivals from Thailand, Cambodia, Laos, Burma and Indonesia in the USA; Algeria and Morocco in Europe (especially France, as both countries are francophone). Economic opportunities, legal and otherwise, brought thousands of new people from Mexico and Central America to the USA. Island people from the Caribbean migrated to the USA and Europe (French-speaking Haitians to France, English-speaking West Indians to the USA and Great Britain). Many technically trained Indians came to work in the

Johann Schott, 'Rosemary' (*Rosmarinus officinalis*), from *Von Dem Nutzen der Dinge* (1518), engraving. Note that this rosemary 'bush' is not planted in the ground – perhaps because, in the frigid North (where the book was written), plants indigenous to sunnier climates were moved to sheltered spots in winter.

exploding computer industry, then found that running food stores or restaurants for their compatriots provided a more stable income than the ever-fluctuating high-tech job market. All of these groups knew coriander and used it routinely in their cooking.

Western cooks noticed. Changes in *lifestyles* (a term that didn't really exist before that time), disposable incomes, levels of education, travel and entertainment media, and a thorough mixing of cultures led to an explosion of interest in what used to be called 'gourmet' cooking. Few people use the term 'gourmet' any more, since today's everyday cooking is more sophisticated than the 'gourmet' cooking of the past.

Coriander could be considered the poster child for all these culturally induced culinary changes. Guacamole and salsa have largely replaced the sour-cream-onion-soupmix dips that were so common a few decades ago. The frozen food aisles of our markets are filled with ready-to-heat meals that would have been impossibly exotic not very long ago: Ecuadorian, Indian, Mexican, Pakistani, Thai and Indonesian dishes compete for shelf space with frozen pot pies and TV dinners. Today, coriander is as common as parsley in the grocery portion of our supermarkets – and no one would even think of substituting one for the other.

Herbs have been with us since before we had agriculture. Regions whose histories have been punctuated by repeated invasions, migrations and colonization have culinary histories that reflect all of those influences. Herbs went along with us, and have changed us, for the most part, more than we have changed them. We are still learning about, and from, these fellow-travellers. A little book like this can only touch on such a large topic, so make use of the resources that follow, in the endmatter, to find out more about these savoury weeds.

Recipes

Herbal Teas

Technically, only tea (*Camellia sinensis*) is brewed to make the beverage of the same name. All the so-called 'herbal teas' are infusions called 'tisanes'. They can be mild, delicate brews made from chamomile or robust quaffs flavoured with fresh rosemary and lemon.

The process is simplicity itself: pour boiling water over the herb of choice, steep until desired strength is achieved, strain and serve. Some of the stronger tasting herbs (rosemary, thyme, mint, bergamot) benefit from a bit of honey.

Other Herbal Beverages

While we have seen that many herbs have been used in brewing beers and complex cordials, they make relatively few appearances in cocktails. Cocktails themselves are a fairly modern invention. There were, of course, punches and syllabubs and similar alcoholic quaffs – but they were always made in large quantities and served by the glass to guests, who all drank the same drink.

The mixtures of spirits with other flavourings (such as fruit juices, sodas of various kinds and garnishes where appropriate), made to order, generally one serving at a time, reflect a greater egalitarianism, individual preferences superseding a style of drinking determined by the host ahead of time. The art of making cocktails really blossomed in the 1920s – which, not coincidentally, was shortly after alcohol was banned in Iceland (1915), Norway (1916), in parts of Canada (1916–19) and of course in the USA by the eighteenth amendment to the Constitution and subsequent Volstead Act (1919). Nothing creates a greater demand for individuality than the imposition of unpopular restrictions on freedom of choice. The cocktail is a perfect example of spontaneous rebellion against authority and a celebration of what was once called 'flaming youth'. Among the now-classic cocktails that made their debuts in the period are Cuba libres and daiquiris (1920), Bloody Marys (1921) and mimosas (1925).

Possibly because of the very newness of cocktails there is little tradition of using fresh herbs in their formulation. One notable exception is mint, which figures prominently in two famous cocktails, both of which pre-date the great flowering of cocktails in the 1920s: the mint julep (first mentioned in print in 1803) and the mojito (a nineteenth-century drink based on much older – seventeenth-century – concoctions). At the time of writing there is a resurgence of interest in cocktails and young mixologists are beginning to experiment with all sorts of new approaches to the bartender's art (such as making flavoured syrups and infused juices). We can expect to see much more in the way of fresh herbs among the traditional mixers and garnishes in the near future.

Blackberry-Rosemary Kir

When combined with bubbly, this syrup makes a surprising herbal variation on a *kir royale*.

2 cups (250 g) fresh blackberries
¼ cup (50 g) sugar
⅓ cup (70 ml) water
1 ½ tablespoons fresh rosemary, finely chopped
1 bottle dry champagne or prosecco
6 orange slices, for garnish

Reserve the six best-looking berries. Combine the remaining berries, sugar, water and rosemary in a small non-reactive saucepan. Simmer for 20 minutes or until slightly thickened. Filter, without pressing, through a fine-mesh strainer. Set aside until cooled.

Divide between six champagne flutes, drop a berry in each, top with the champagne or prosecco, place an orange slice on each glass and serve.

Makes enough for 6 cocktails

Elderberry Blossom Syrup

This fragrant syrup can be used in cocktails, added to prosecco or mixed with seltzer for a refreshing non-alcoholic quaff. Pour it over sliced fresh strawberries and allow the flavours to develop for at least half an hour before serving.

20 elderflower heads, collected before noon
1 lemon, sliced
2 teaspoons Ball Fruit Fresh (see note)
2 kg (4½ lb) white sugar
1 200 ml (1 quart + 1 cup) boiling water

Trim flowers of all stems, and pick over to discard insects, leaves or other debris. Place in a large bowl with sugar, lemon and Ball Fruit Fresh. Pour boiling water over the dry ingredients. Stir until the sugar has dissolved. Cover with plastic wrap. Stir twice a day for five days.

Strain though a bouillon strainer and/or through a moistened clean cloth napkin. Fill sterile bottles or canning jars. Refrigerate or, if using canning jars, seal and process in a canner for 15 minutes.

Note: Ball Fruit Fresh is a mixture of ascorbic acid (vitamin C) and citric acid, used to prevent browning due to oxidation and preserve the colour of fresh fruits and vegetables when cut.

Makes about 3 pints

Additional Herbal Recipes

Cucumber-Shiso Pickles

This is typical of Japanese pickled (but unfermented) vegetable dishes, collectively known as *sunomono* – cool and refreshing, they can be used as a light appetizer or to accompany rice or noodles.

½ cup (120 ml) unseasoned rice wine vinegar
3 tablespoons mirin
¼ cup (50 g) sugar
1 tablespoon sea salt
1 cup (175 g) cucumbers, thinly sliced
1 cup (175 g) daikon (Japanese radish) or young red radishes,
thinly sliced
8 red perilla leaves

Make a marinade of the first four ingredients in a non-reactive bowl. Stir until all solids are dissolved. Slice the perilla into fine shreds (like a basil chiffonade). Combine all ingredients in a non-reactive bowl, cover and refrigerate overnight.

Serve pickles ice cold.

Makes 2 cups, or approximately 500 g

Michigan Corn Chowder

We had this soup in a small roadside cafe near Lake Michigan and not far from the Indiana border. It's light yet satisfying, very flavourful, not at all heavy handed with the cream and so impressive that we asked our server about the recipe. Unfortunately she told us that the chef 'never tells anyone what he does in his kitchen', so this is merely an attempt to recreate it. The secret, of course, is the subtle and unexpected tang of lemongrass.

950 ml (1 quart) good chicken stock
1 stalk fresh lemongrass, chopped
3 ears fresh corn
1 sweet red pepper, seeded and chopped to size of corn kernels
1 small onion chopped to size of corn kernels
salt and pepper to taste
1 teaspoon Italian parsley, chopped
1 tablespoon double (heavy) cream

Combine lemongrass and stock, simmer for 20 minutes (until the stock is well flavoured). Strain the stock and reserve, discarding the lemongrass.

Cut kernels from cobs, then scrape the cobs with edge of knife to extract all the milky fluid from the base of the kernels. Add corn, red pepper and onions to stock; simmer until vegetables are tender.

Add cream and parsley, adjust seasoning and serve.

Serves 4

Roasted Loin of Pork with Za'atar and Caramelized Garlic

This roast comes to the table with a gleaming, nearly black, glaze. The interior of the pork, however, is juicy and elegantly white by contrast. The amount of caramelized garlic may seem too much for four to six people but poaching in sherry removes most of the garlic's unpleasant sulphur compounds and the final browning renders them sweet and silken, almost unctuous.

2 tablespoons pomegranate molasses (see notes)
2 tablespoons honey
1 tablespoon olive oil (not extra virgin)
½ teaspoon za'atar, crumbled (see notes)
¼ teaspoon freshly ground black pepper
1 clove garlic, mashed to a paste
2 large heads of garlic, separated into cloves, but not peeled
1.3–1.8 kg (3–4 lb) boneless loin of pork
1 cup (225 ml) dry sherry

Combine the first six ingredients in a large non-reactive bowl (or resealable plastic bag large enough to hold the pork loin) to make the marinade. Spread the marinade over the pork loin, making sure all sides are covered. Marinate eight hours (or overnight) in refrigerator, turning three or four times in the marinade.

Preheat oven to 175°C/350°F. Rub a little olive oil in a roasting pan, add the pork loin and roast for 60 to 75 minutes, basting frequently. When the internal temperature reaches 70°C/160°F, remove from the oven, cover with aluminum foil (the temperature will continue to rise to a safe 74°C/165°F, and the meat will neither dry out nor shrink). It should rest, covered in a warm place, for about 15 minutes – just enough time to prepare the caramelized garlic.

When the roast comes out of the oven, bring the sherry to a boil in a small saucepan. Poach the garlic cloves in sherry for 2 minutes. Drain them, discarding the sherry. Peel the cloves (cutting off the blunt stem end with a paring knife should allow the skins to slip right off). Sauté the drained, dried garlic cloves in the olive oil, tossing frequently until evenly golden brown and deeply fragrant. Serve as a garnish with slices of the roast.

Notes: Pomegranate molasses is not molasses at all, but an astringent reduction of tart pomegranate juice. It can be found in markets that carry Middle Eastern products. There's no real substitute but tamarind extract is an approximation.

Za'atar is a generic name for a number of Middle Eastern herbs (*Origanum cyriacum*, *Thymus capitatus* and *Thymbra spicata*, among others). Its flavour and aroma are reminiscent of thyme, oregano and marjoram, and a mixture of two or more of these would make an adequate substitute. However, be careful not to substitute *zathar*, which is a spice mixture usually containing thyme and sumac, and sometimes sesame and other ingredients.

Serves four to six, generously

Basil-scented Strawberries

Very familiar fruits, like strawberries, can be enhanced by a little unexpected edge (such as the now-classic addition of black pepper). In this recipe the subtle clove–anise taste of fresh basil adds an almost tropical mystique to a family favourite.

225 ml (1 cup) water
200 g (1 cup) sugar
20 g (¼ cup) fresh basil leaves, chopped
2 pints (500 g) fresh strawberries, hulled and sliced
4 perfect basil leaves, whole

Combine water and sugar in sauce pot, heat until all sugar is dissolved. Remove from heat. Add chopped basil, stir, then set aside to cool.

When completely cooled, strain syrup through cheesecloth (or a chinoise) to remove all particles of spent basil. Pour over strawberries and place in refrigerator, covered, for at least an hour to allow flavours to merge.

Divide the berries into four portions, garnish with reserved whole basil leaves and serve.

Serves 4

Rosemary Shortbread

65 g (½ cup) cornmeal
210 g (1½ cups) plain (all-purpose) flour
100 g (½ cup) sugar
1 tablespoon fresh rosemary, finely chopped
1 rounded teaspoon salt
1½ tablespoons dark honey (such as buckwheat or loosestrife)
220 g (2 sticks) ice cold, unsalted butter, cut into small chunks

Preheat oven to 160°C / 325°F.

Briefly pulse cornmeal, flour, sugar, rosemary and salt in the bowl of a food processor until combined. Add butter and honey and pulse until mixture forms crumbs and just begins to come together (don't process too much, or gluten will develop in the dough, resulting in a tough chewy product).

Press dough with the side of your thumb into an ungreased 20-cm (9-inch)-square baking pan. Prick dough all over with a fork. Bake for 35 to 40 minutes until golden brown.

Partly cool on a wire rack – but cut into desired shapes before it's completely cooled, or it will shatter.

Makes one 9-inch shortbread

Thyme-scented Fruit Salad

2 tablespoons almond oil
1 tablespoon fresh thyme leaves
1 tablespoon honey
1 lemon, juice and zest
1 teaspoon white wine vinegar
salt and freshly cracked black pepper
½ honeydew melon, deseeded and cut into balls
½ cantaloupe, deseeded and cut into balls
2 cups (250 g) red seedless grapes

Combine oil, thyme leaves, honey, lemon zest and juice, and vinegar in a small bowl. Whisk until the ingredients are well-mixed. Taste and adjust seasoning with salt and pepper.

Toss fruits with dressing and serve.

Makes 4–5 cups

Raw Tomato Sauce

For 450 g/1 lb cooked pasta
This is an ideal summer dish – made when tomatoes are most flavourful, and a sauce that doesn't require long cooking is most appreciated!

60 ml (¼ cup) good fruity olive oil
1 small shallot, peeled and minced
1 tablespoon fresh tarragon leaves, chopped (plus a sprig for garnish)
450 g (1 lb) ripe tomatoes, peeled, seeded and chopped
salt and freshly cracked black pepper

Combine first four ingredients (except garnish) in a non-reactive bowl, cover and allow flavours to meld, at least an hour. Purée the sauce (in blender or through a food mill). Taste and adjust seasoning with salt and pepper.

Toss with cooked pasta, garnish with sprig of tarragon and serve.

Serves 4

References

Introduction

1 Susan Weingarten, 'Wild Foods in the Talmud: The Influence of Religious Restrictions on Consumption', in *Wild Food: Proceedings of the Oxford Symposium on Food and Cookery 2004* (Devon, 2006), pp. 323–3.
2 Gary Allen, *The Herbalist in the Kitchen* (Urbana, IL, 2007), p. 224.

1 What, Exactly, are Herbs?

1 Gary Allen, *The Herbalist in the Kitchen* (Urbana, IL, 2007), p. 8.

2 The Usual Suspects

1 Jean Bottéro, *The Oldest Cuisine in the World: Cooking in Mesopotamia* (Chicago, IL, 2004), p. 3.
2 Ibid.
3 Stephen Bertman, *Handbook of Life in Ancient Mesopotamia* (New York, 2003), pp. 291–3.
4 Bottéro, *The Oldest Cuisine in the World*, pp. 69, 71.
5 Paul Freedman, ed., *Food: The History of Taste* (Berkeley and Los Angeles, CA, 2007), p. 59.

6 Pliny the Elder, *Natural History*, book XIX, chapter 57, ed. John Bostock and H. T. Riley (London, 1855).

7 Agnes Robertson Arber, *Herbals, their Origin and Evolution* (Cambridge, 1938), pp. 44–5.

8 Ibid., pp. 52–66, 74–5.

9 Ibid., p. 70.

10 Ibid., pp. 72–4.

11 Quoted by Alice Ross, in 'Sallets', available at www. journalofantiques.com, accessed March 2011.

12 Nicholas Culpeper, 'Original Epistle to the Reader', in *Complete Herbal* (1653), available at www.bibliomania.com, accessed March 2011.

13 Debs Cook, 'The Royal Herb Strewer', available at http:// herbsociety.org.uk, accessed March 2011.

14 Pliny, *Natural History*, Book XIX, chap. 36.

15 Ibid., Book XIX, chap. 32.

16 Ibid., Book XIX, chap. 47.

17 Ibid., Book XIX, chap. 55.

18 Ibid., Book XIX, chap. 54.

19 Ibid., Book XIX, chap. 33.

20 Ibid., Book IV, chap. 50.

21 Culpeper, 'Garden Bazil, or Sweet Bazil', in *Complete Herbal*.

22 Ibid., 'The Bay Tree', 'Sweet Marjoram', 'Winter and Summer Savoury'.

23 Ibid., 'Mint'.

24 Ibid., 'Mustard'.

25 Ibid., 'Thyme'.

26 Ibid., 'Dill'.

27 Ibid., 'Cives'.

28 Ibid., 'Water Cresses'.

29 Pliny, *Natural History*, Book XIX, chap. 44.

30 Culpepper, 'Angelica', in *Complete Herbal*.

31 Richard LeStrange, *A History of Herbal Plants* (New York, 1977), p. 138.

32 Lise Manniche, *An American Egyptian Herbal* (London, 2006), p. 83.

33 Craig Claiborne, *An Herb and Spice Cook Book* (New York, 1963), p. 319.

34 Alexander and Zhenia Fleisher, 'Identification of Biblical Hyssop and Origin of the Traditional Use of Oregano-group Herbs in the Mediterranean Region', *Economic Botany*, 42 (1988), pp. 232–41.

35 Samuel Pepys, *The Diary of Samuel Pepys* (New York and London, 1953), p. 141.

36 Pliny, *Natural History*, Book XIX, chap. 44.

37 Culpeper, 'Borage and Bugloss', in *Complete Herbal*.

38 Pliny, *Natural History*, Book XIX, chap. 38.

39 Ibid., Book XIX, chap. 19.

40 Note that the Latin of the Middle Ages was neither classic, nor that of modern science.

41 Quoted in Laura L. Howes, *Chaucer's Gardens and the Language of Convention* (Gainesville, FL, 1997), p. 22.

42 Eleanour Sinclair Rohde, *The Old English Herbals* (London and New York, 1922), p. 1.

3 A Less Eurocentric Herbarium

1 National Research Council, *Lost Crops of Africa*, vol. II: *Vegetables* (Washington, DC, 2006), p. 78, accessed March 2011.

2 Haroun Hallack, personal communication. Hallack worked as an extension agent in Sierra Leone, and now teaches sustainable agricultural practices at Redbud Farm in Berkeley County, West Virginia.

3 National Research Council, *Lost Crops of Africa*, vol. II: *Vegetables*, p. 93.

4 Diana Buja, 'African Honey Wine Recipes, 1862', at http://dianbuja.wordpress.com, accessed 25 October 2011.

5 'Food: Bread, Beer, and All Good Things', available at www.reshafim.org.il, accessed March 2011.

6 Tadeuz Lewicki, *West African Food in the Middle Ages* (Cambridge, 1974), pp. 57, 67, 219.

7 Ibid.

8 Gary Allen, *The Herbalist in the Kitchen* (Urbana, IL, 2007), p. 156.
9 Richard LeStrange, *A History of Herbal Plants* (New York, 1977), p. 115.

4 The Sisterhood of the Travelling Plants

1 Richard Hakluyt et al., *Divers Voyages Touching the Discovery of America and the Islands Adjacent* (London, 1850), p. 127.
2 'Emigrant Ship Provisions List 1630', available at www.pilgrimhall.org, accessed March 2011.
3 Donna R. Barnes and Peter G. Rose, *Matters of Taste: Food and Drink in Seventeenth-Century Dutch Art and Life* (Syracuse, NY, 2002), p. 23; Peter G. Rose, *Food, Drink and Celebrations of the Hudson Valley Dutch* (Charleston, SC, and London, 2009) and *Matters of Taste: Dutch Recipes with an American Connection* (Syracuse, NY, 2002).
4 John Custis, *The Letterbook of John Custis IV of Williamsburg, 1717–1742* (Lanham, MD, 2005), pp. 197–8.
5 Donald Culross Peattie, *Green Laurels: The Lives and Achievements of the Great Naturalists* (New York, 1936), p. 189.
6 One specimen he discovered in the mountains of Georgia (*Franklinia alatamaha*), named for his friend Benjamin Franklin, has never been found again in the wild. Every living specimen is descended from the cuttings he propagated.
7 Joseph Kastner, *A Species of Eternity* (New York, 1977), p. 62.
8 US Department of Agriculture, 'Invasive and Noxious Weeds', available at http://plants.usda.gov, accessed March 2011.
9 Richard LeStrange, *A History of Herbal Plants* (New York, 1977), p. 58.
10 Ibid., p. 64.
11 Ibid., p. 215.
12 Ibid., p. 37.
13 National Research Council, *Lost Crops of Africa*, vol. II: *Vegetables* (Washington, DC, 2006), pp. 248–50.

Bibliography

Allen, Gary, *The Herbalist in the Kitchen* (Urbana, IL, 2007)
Arber, Agnes Robertson, *Herbals, their Origin and Evolution*
    (Cambridge, 1938)
Bailey, L. H., *Hortus Third: A Concise Dictionary of Plants Cultivated*
    in the United States and Canada (New York, 1976)
Barnes, Donna R., and Peter G. Rose, *Matters of Taste: Food and*
    Drink in Seventeenth-Century Dutch Art and Life (Syracuse,
    NY, 2002)
Bertman, Stephen, *Handbook of Life in Ancient Mesopotamia*
    (New York, 2003)
Bottéro, Jean, *The Oldest Cuisine in the World: Cooking in*
    Mesopotamia (Chicago, IL, 2004)
Brown, Jane, *Vita's Other World: A Gardening Biography of*
    V. Sackville-West (Harmondsworth, 1985)
Buja, Diana, 'African Honey Wine Recipes, 1862', available at
    http://dianabuja.wordpress.com, accessed March 2011
Claiborne, Craig, *An Herb and Spice Cookbook* (New York, 1963)
Collins, Minta, *Medieval Herbals: The Illustrative Traditions*
    (Toronto, 2000)
Conrad, Barnaby III, *Absinthe, History in a Bottle* (San Francisco,
    CA, 1988)
Corn, Charles, *The Scents of Eden: A Narrative of the Spice Trade*
    (New York, Tokyo and London, 1998)
Custis, John, *The Letterbook of John Custis IV of Williamsburg,*
    1717–1742 (Lanham, MD, 2005)

Dalby, Andrew, *Siren Feasts: A History of Food and Gastronomy in Greece* (London and New York, 1997)

Facciola, Stephen, *Cornucopia II, A Sourcebook of Edible Plants* (Vista, CA, 1999)

Fleisher, Alexander, and Zhenia Fleisher, 'Identification of Biblical Hyssop and Origin of the Traditional Use of Oregano-group Herbs in the Mediterranean Region', *Economic Botany*, 42 (1988), pp. 232–41

Freedman, Paul, ed., *Food: The History of Taste* (Berkeley and Los Angeles, CA, 2007)

Freeman, Margaret B., *Herbs for the Medieval Household, for Cooking, Healing and Divers Uses* (New York, 1943)

Grieve, Mrs M., *A Modern Herbal* (London, 1931)

Hakluyt, Richard, et al., *Divers Voyages Touching the Discovery of America and the Islands Adjacent* (London, 1850)

Harrop, Renny, ed., *Encyclopedia of Herbs* (London and New York, 1977)

Hedrick, U. P., ed., *Sturtevant's Edible Plants of the World* [1919] (New York, 1972)

Holland, B., et al. *Vegetables, Herbs and Spices* (Cambridge, 1991)

Howes, Laura L., *Chaucer's Gardens and the Language of Convention* (Gainesville, FL, 1997)

Hutchins, Alma, *A Handbook of Native American Herbs* (Boston, MA, 1992)

—, *Indian Herbology of North America* (Boston, MA, 1991)

Hutton, Wendy, *Tropical Herbs and Spices* (Singapore, 1997)

Johns, Timothy, *With Bitter Herbs They Shall Eat It: Chemical Ecology and the Origins of Human Diet and Medicine* (Tucson, AZ, 1960)

Kastner, Joseph, *A Species of Eternity* (New York, 1977)

Keville, Kathi, *The Illustrated Herb Encyclopedia* (New York, 1991)

Keay, John, *The Spice Route: A History* (Berkeley, CA, 2006)

LaTorre, Dolores L., *Cooking and Curing with Mexican Herbs* (Austin, TX, 1977)

Laudan, Rachel, *The Food of Paradise: Exploring Hawaii's Culinary Heritage* (Honolulu, HI, 1996)

LeStrange, Richard, *A History of Herbal Plants* (New York, 1977)

Lewicki, Tadeuz, *West African Food in the Middle Ages* (Cambridge, 1974)

Linares, Edelmira and Judith Aguirre, eds, *Los Quelites, un Tesoro Culinario* (México, 1992)

Manniche, Lise, *An Egyptian Herbal* (London, 2006)

Miller, Richard Alan, *The Magical and Ritual Use of Aphrodisiacs* (Rochester, VT, 1985)

Murai, M., F. Pen and C. D. Miller, *Some Tropical South Pacific Island Foods; Description, History, Use, Composition, and Nutritive Value* (Honolulu, HI, 1958)

Nichols, Rose Standish, *English Pleasure Gardens* (Boston, MA, 2003)

Northcote, Rosalind Lucy, *The Book of Herb Lore* (New York, 1971; reprint of *The Book of Herbs*, 1912)

Ortiz, Elisabeth Lambert, *The Encyclopedia of Herbs, Spices and Flavorings* (New York, 1992)

Owen, Sri, *Indonesian Food* (London, 2008)

Passmore, Jacki, *The Encyclopedia of Asian Food and Cooking* (New York, 1991)

Peattie, Donald Culross, *Green Laurels: The Lives and Achievements of the Great Naturalists* (New York, 1936)

Pepys, Samuel, *The Diary of Samuel Pepys* (New York and London, 1953)

Rätsch, Christian, *The Dictionary of Sacred and Magical Plants* (Santa Barbara, CA, 1992)

Reilly, Ann, ed., *Taylor's Pocket Guide to Herbs and Edible Flowers* (Boston, MA, 1990)

Rohde, Eleanour Sinclair, *Culinary and Salad Herbs, Their Cultivation and Food Values with Recipes* [1940] (New York, 1972)

—, *The Old English Herbals* (New York and London, 1922)

Root, Waverley, ed., *Herbs and Spices, The Pursuit of Flavor* (New York, 1980)

Schneider, Elizabeth, *Uncommon Fruits and Vegetables* (New York, 1986)

Shaudys, Phyllis V., *Herbal Treasures* (Pownal, VT, 1990)

Seidemann, Johannes, *World Spice Plants* (Berlin, 2005)

Sokolov, Raymond, *Why We Eat What We Eat* (New York, 1991)

Staples, George W. and Michael S. Kristiansen, *Ethnic Culinary Herbs: A Guide to Identification and Cultivation in Hawai'i* (Honolulu, HI, 1999)

Stuart, Malcolm, ed., *The Encyclopedia of Herbs and Herbalism* (New York, 1979)

Von Reis, Siri, *Drugs and Foods from Little Known Plants (notes in Harvard University Herbaria)* (Cambridge, MA, 1973)

—, 'Exploring the Herbarium', *Scientific American* (May 1977), pp. 96–104

Weatherford, Jack, *Indian Givers: How the Indians of the Americas Transformed the World* (New York, 1988)

Weingarten, Susan, 'Wild Foods in the Talmud: The Influence of Religious Restrictions on Consumption', in *Wild Food: Proceedings of the Oxford Symposium on Food and Cookery 2004* (Devon, 2006)

Witty, Helen, ed., *Billy Joe Tatum's Wild Foods Cookbook and Field Guide* (New York, 1976)

Wolfert, Paula, *Mediterranean Grains and Greens* (New York, 1998)

—, *The Cooking of the Eastern Mediterranean* (New York, 1994)

—, *Couscous and Other Good Food from Morocco* (New York, 1973)

Websites and Associations

Botanical research

Arnold Arboretum
www.arboretum.harvard.edu

Botany Libraries/Gray Herbarium Libraries/Economic Botany
www.huh.harvard.edu

Ethnobotany.com
www.ethnobotany.com

Fernwood Botanic Garden
www.fernwoodbotanical.org

Herb Research News
www.herbs.org

New York Botanical Garden
www.nybg.org

Herb history

Las Hierbas de Cocina
http://mexconnect.com

Latin Wordlist of Assorted Herbs, Spices, Plants &
Miscellaneous Foodstuffs
www.chebucto.ns.ca

Ps. Apuleius, Herbal, England, St Augustine's abbey,
Canterbury; *c.* 1070–1100
www.bodley.ox.ac.uk

Ps. Apuleius, Dioscorides, Herbals (extracts); De virtutibus
bestiarum in arte medicinae, in Latin and English, England,
Bury St Edmunds; 11th century
www.bodley.ox.ac.uk

University of Florida Herbarium Library
www.flmnh.ufl.edu

Societies and associations

American Botanical Council
www.herbalgram.org

American Herb Association
www.ahaherb.com

American Herbalists Guild
www.americanherbalistsguild.com

Arizona Herb Association
www.azherb.org

Canadian Herb Society
www.herbsociety.ca

Herb Society
www.herbsociety.co.uk

Herb Society of America
www.herbsociety.org

Herb Society of Central Florida
www.floridaplants.com

Herb Society of Southwestern Virginia
http://dir.gardenweb.com

International Herb Association
www.iherb.org

Massachusetts Horticultural Society
www.masshort.org

Resources for herb enthusiasts

Gernot Katzer's Spice Pages
www-ang.kfunigraz.ac.at

Herb Companion
www.herbcompanion.com

Herb Quarterly
www.herbquarterly.com

Kräuterlexikon
www.heilkraeuter.de

Seeds

Herbs Australia
www.screamingseeds.com.au

Native American Seed
www.seedsource.com

Native Seeds
www.nativeseeds.org

Acknowledgements

A book like this is the product of the expertise and support of many people. They deserve all the credit for its strengths – the blame for its weaknesses I reserve for myself.

I have to thank former colleagues at The Culinary Institute of America, whose collective culinary experience and generosity of spirit always exceeded even my greediest expectations espe cially Bob Delgrosso, Steven Kolpan, Krishnendu Ray, Konstantin Sembos and Jonathan Zearfoss.

A book like this would have been impossible without the assistance of libraries and I spent many happy hours in The Conrad Hilton Library of The Culinary Institute of America, The Massachusetts Horticultural Society Library, The Sojourner Truth Library of the State University of New York College at New Paltz and The New York Public Library. I took most of the photos at The Brooklyn Botanical Gardens, The Chicago Botanical Gardens, the herb garden at of The Culinary Institute of America, The Phantom Gardener in Rhinebeck, New York, and the Robison York State Herb Garden at Cornell University.

I am indebted for the generous contributions of Ken Albala, Diana Buja, Nancy Harmon Jenkins, Rachel Laudan, Jacqueline Newman, Andrew Smith, Paula Wolfert, Clifford Wright and numerous members of the Association for the Study of Food and Society, who never failed to provide answers when I couldn't find them myself.

Deborah Begley and Tamara Watson not only plied me with great food and wine, but delivered them with wit and intelligence.

So many others should be listed here that – had they been included a second volume would have been required. Nonetheless, I would be a fool if I did not acknowledge the contributions of my wife, Karen, whose support and wry humour, tempered by wholly justified scepticism – not to mention her willingness to try, *once*, whatever weird things appeared on our table – made this book possible.

Photo Acknowledgements

The author and the publishers wish to express their thanks to the below sources of illustrative material and/or permission to reproduce it:

Gary Allen: pp. 10, 11, 17, 37, 39, 40, 41, 43, 44, 47, 51, 54, 57, 76, 80, 83, 87, 90, 101, 108, 110, 115, 117, 118; Istockphoto: p. 6 (Lezh); Rex Features: p. 34 (Roger-Viollet); Werner Forman Archive: p. 124 (Oriental Collection, State University Library, Leiden).

Index

italic numbers refer to illustrations; **bold** to recipes